Audition

Audition

Everything an Actor Needs to Know to Get the Part

Michael Shurtleff

Walker and Company

New York

First published in the United States of America
in 1978 by the Walker Publishing Company, Inc.

Published simultaneously in Canada by Beaverbooks,
Limited, Pickering, Ontario

ISBN: 0-8027-0590-1

Library of Congress Catalog Card Number 77-90134

Printed in the United States of America

THIRTEENTH PRINTING

to Onna and to Keith

Contents

My thanks go to two remarkable Broadway producers, Stuart Ostrow and David Merrick, for their belief in me and for the inimitable opportunities they gave me to learn.

Foreword

I have never written a foreword before, so I have no knowledge of
its purpose. I called a few of my more literate friends and asked
them: Exactly what should a foreword accomplish? Their general
consensus was that it should predict in some way or other a little of
what the reader might expect to follow. That sounds reasonable
enough, but I sensed it was incomplete. I always tend to feel my
friends are misleading me—or at least telling me only part of what
I should know. Of course, you can only expect that from your closest
friends.

Therefore, I read a few forewords to several "How To" books
and even to some novels. I didn't learn too much from them. On the
contrary, I found most of them too long, too academic, or, in some
cases, as if the writer of the foreword was in competition with the
writer of the book and was trying to out-write him—so to speak. It
was a little like a five-round preliminary writing bout. The foreword
writer would swing a left obscure verb to the jaw and shortly follow
with a seven syllable adjective—one that would immediately send
me running to the nearest fat dictionary.

Feeling I wanted nothing to do with any of these approaches,
I was forced to do my own thinking (something I try to postpone as
long as possible) about what I would like to say about Michael Shurtleff and this book.

First off, I would like to go on record as saying that I consider
this book to be *absolutely indispensable* to any aspiring, or even
mildly ambitious, actor. There is NO book of which I am aware that
gives an actor such first-rate, clear-cut, no-nonsense advice. God
knows there have been a goodly supply of books written about acting
and the theatre, but none that I've read are so usefully straightforward and practical as this one.

I have seen many talented actors not get hired simply because
of a poor audition. It happens all too frequently in the theatre and
in films, too.

Michael explains to the reader all the possible situations and
predicaments an actor might expect. Most importantly, he explains
clearly how to deal with them. He even goes into such details as
dress. Not important, you say? Oh, no? Well, read on.

Although the book is directed to helping actors audition successfully (by that I mean gain employment—get the part—something

which is extremely difficult in today's market; is it 80 or 90 percent of Actor's Equity who are unemployed?), I began to think that with a little imagination, a little transcribing in the reader's mind, how useful this book can be to people outside the theatre. After all, isn't a business interview an audition in a way? Isn't a first date? In today's world everything seems like some sort of long audition to me.

Now I'd like to say a few words about the author, Michael Shurtleff. I hope he doesn't read this because I'm sure he would be embarrassed by my affection and admiration for him. I know no man I trust more in the theatre. Whenever I'm undecided about script, actors or anything pertaining to a show or a movie, I know I can always turn to Michael, ask his opinion and get an honest, no-bullshit answer. In a business where most are playing it cautiously, just "in case" something should go wrong, this is indeed a rare quality.

He has probably seen more actors audition than anyone in the theatre today. He has been instrumental—and sometimes totally responsible—for getting more unknown actors their break than anyone I know.

He is a totally dedicated man. In the past fifteen years or so, I think he has seen just about every play or musical on Broadway, Off Broadway, Off-Off Broadway, those done in lofts, studios, backs of stores and, I'm sure, even in living rooms. He loves actors (something not always easy to do; but Michael does care about them). Many times at a casting session, I have seen him wince in pain after a particular actor or actress had done a bad or mediocre audition. Noticing his expression (which really isn't accurately a "wince," since Michael doesn't "wince;" but he does have an expression that comes close and could pass for a wince), I would ask, "Why?" He would painfully reply, "I don't know why that actor did it that way. He's really talented. Doesn't he realize he just did himself in?" Then, after a pause, "Couldn't you read him again?" Most usually I would. I *do* trust his instincts.

There was no doubt Michael's pain was sincere. I imagine that pain and his desire to help young actors is what motivated the writing of this book.

There is one other of Michael's many attributes I think worthy of mention. At least I found it unusual. As a casting director, he was always looking for and desperately trying to help the director find the "off-beat" actor. The one that you wouldn't ordinarily cast in that role, but one that has some very special quality—a quality that just might turn an ordinary part into a brilliant one. Michael has a keen eye for spotting just such an actor. Of course, it is not always easy to sell the "off-beat" casting idea to a director. They generally tend toward typecasting. Not me, of course, but those other fellows.

I believe I have said enough. Oh, yes, just one other thing: Because of my aforementioned affection for Michael, I would like his book to sell; *and* being somewhat aware of today's tastes, I thought I should make mention of the rather explicit erotic passages near the end of the book. Just because Michael is always honest doesn't mean I have to be.

—BOB FOSSE

Prologue

Is it generally known that an actor's life is a difficult one—not glamorous, most of the time, and filled with disappointment and rejection and hard work? We who spend our lives working in the theatre know this so well that we may mistakenly assume the rest of the world knows, too. Yet clearly not, or no one would come from the ranks of civilian life to enlist in the world of acting. Many do. The dream still exists: one's name up in lights, one's face up there on that giant screen, the adoration of the public, great romance, fame and glory.

The truth is that for every actor who gets hired for a part, fifty or a hundred or two hundred do not. An actor is forever trying to get a part; an actor is forever getting rejected, never knowing why, simply not wanted. An actor's life is not to be envied. It consists mostly of losing out, of being turned down. Unendurable, such a life, for most of us. I will never know how actors manage to persist.

Several times a week, sometimes several times a day in the case of commercials, an actor has to go try out for a job. This means he must do a *reading*, that is, he must take a scene from the script, look it over, and get up and give a performance. Yet for all his years of study, training, and experience in community theatre, college theatre, stock, regional, Off-Off-Broadway, Off Broadway, even on Broadway, nothing in the actor's life prepares him for this endless— for most, lifelong—process of auditioning to try to get a role.

For in order to act, it is necessary to audition for the role—unless you are a star or a great and good friend of the director. If it is a musical, the audition entails singing, perhaps dancing, and then reading for the role. If it is a straight play, there may be an initial interview, but everything hangs on your reading for the role. Since an actor's life is made up of auditions, why does nothing in his training prepare him to audition? What is he to do in order to get the job?

Actors take classes. Actors train, just as dancers or musicians do. There are those few who regard themselves as "naturals," not to be interfered with by awareness of craft, but most actors know they need a craft and must acquire a technique. Acting is a small part inspiration (and very welcome, that) but mostly hard work. Yet all the training in the world can go for naught if the actor in the reading situation can't convince the auditors he can perform the role.

Many a well-known actor has said that if he or she had to audition, they would never get the job. That was Ruth Gordon's contention to me, and so said Katherine Cornell. I doubt that is true, however; it means they're fortunate in never having to audition, but if faced with this necessity, they would be expert and imaginative enough to find a way. What they do mean is that the task of doing readings is a terrifying one. It's not the same as performing. It's a different skill the actor must acquire.

This book tells you how.

II.

It all began when I was casting the Broadway production of THE LION IN WINTER. This was, of course, long before Katharine Hepburn and Peter O'Toole illuminated the wit and the passion of Jim Goldman's characters in the film version, so the New York actors who came in to audition for the play had no precedent, and they read as they usually, and unfortunately, do for "historical" plays: straightforward, earnest, loud. After three weeks of this, the English director, Noel Willman, turned to me and asked, "Don't American actors have any sense of humor at all?"

Surely, I thought, American actors have a sense of humor! Someone must teach them to use their humor. I started in to teach.

I had for many years been a casting director for Broadway plays (among them BECKET with Laurence Olivier and Anthony Quinn, GYPSY with Ethel Merman, ROSENCRANTZ AND GUILDENSTERN ARE DEAD, CARNIVAL, PIPPIN, THE ODD COUPLE, CHICAGO, A TASTE OF HONEY) and films (THE SOUND OF MUSIC, JESUS CHRIST SUPERSTAR, 1776, THE SAND PEBBLES, ALL THE WAY HOME, THE GRADUATE), and my work included seeing actors perform in the many places actors do plays in New York: churches, coffeehouses, bars, basements, lofts, little theatres upstairs, little theatres downstairs, ELT (Equity Library Theatre), Off Broadway, on Broadway, everywhere. I usually went to the theatre eight or nine times a week; weekends I'd sometimes see as many as five or six performances Off-Off-Broadway. Since what I saw the actor do in performance was so frequently *not* what he did when I had him in to audition for a Broadway production or a film, it was clear that the actor did not know what was required of him in the reading situation. Particularly with regard to humor.

I started out to teach actors to find the humor in the role they were reading for. But since humor can't be isolated but can only be found in exploring character and situation, I evolved the *twelve guideposts* to help an actor to use himself well in the audition situation. Since they work in the audition process, they work in the actor's rehearsal and performing life as well.

There are no rules for the creative act—it is the exception to the rule that interests us the most—but there are definite questions that the auditioning actor should ask himself. The *answers* to the questions posed by the guideposts will be different for every human being who asks them, since no two of us are alike. If we presume that actors are even more disparate and nonconforming than other human beings—why else would they be actors?—then the answers they come up with can be unique.

Actors don't trust this. Actors, who should pride themselves on their singularity, are forever trying to be someone else. It isn't necessary for you, the actor, to like yourself—self-love isn't easy come by for most of us—but you must learn to trust who you are. There is no one else like you.

The guideposts are questions for the actor to ask. They are not rules. They are not a technique. They are to guide an actor to his feelings. There is little else an actor can use as source material in a reading but his own emotional life.

For some years I have taught these guideposts in my classes on How to Audition. Actors tell me that the twelve guideposts provide an organized and functional approach not only to auditioning but to all of their acting life as well: a synthesis of all the training and experience an actor undergoes in his life's work. The guideposts deny none of an actor's previous training; rather they give him a functional way to apply all of it to the practical everyday task of getting a job. And how to work on and perform the part once he has it.

III.

To go into acting is like asking for admission to an insane asylum. Anyone may apply, but only the certifiably insane are admitted. In my actor card file are fifty thousand actors. I would hazard to say about five hundred of them earn a living acting. And a large part of their income comes from doing commercials, which is not exactly acting, is it? So it's clear, right off the bat, that from any rational point of view, to become an actor is an act of insanity. Why would one go into a profession in which it is nigh onto impossible to earn a living?

It's filled with ironies, the profession of acting. Most people go into acting to get out of themselves, to get away from their everyday humdrum selves and become someone else who is glamorous, romantic, unusual, different. And what does acting turn out to be? Using your own self. Working from what's inside you. Not being someone else, but being you in different situations and contexts. Not escaping you, but using yourself naked and exposed up there on the stage or the silver screen.

I've always thought it's better to give up sanity. Settle down and admit you're crazy or you wouldn't want to act. When you find out what acting is like and what the odds are, and you still persist, the proof of your own insanity is inescapable. Accept it. Most actors make themselves unhappy by searching for sanity, by insisting on their normalcy; it's a grave mistake. The life of an actor is a bit easier to take if you admit you're bonkers.

But the admission of insanity is no escape from the hard road ahead, which is learning to use yourself when you act without putting any limitations on who you are. Actors are, among their more pronounced idiosyncrasies, addicted to talking about their "characters." "I play this character who goes mad in the second act" or "My character is a devoted husband and father; he'd never be tempted by another woman." Actors waste a lot of audition time thinking about their "character," which often means running away from the very use of themselves that is needed. Audition time is precious. You are given very little of it, not enough to undertake a search for this other character. The pressure is such that the "character" must come from inside the actor—immediately.

The first change to undertake from your performing method in learning how to audition is to give up character and use yourself.

In teaching my How to Audition classes, I find the success of the actor in auditioning is in direct ratio to his willingness to give up searching for another character and to use himself. Think on it: it takes weeks of delving in rehearsal to mold a "character." How can you achieve that when you have the script overnight or, as is so often the case in the Broadway theatre, when you only have ten or fifteen minutes to look at a scene before you go out to read it in front of the auditors. In ten minutes you're going to whip up a fully grown character? No way.

Learn to use yourself.

Don't misunderstand what I mean by *yourself*. I don't mean your everyday real self, for plays are not written about those everyday circumstances but about *unusual* predicaments, where what happens is out of the ordinary; so it naturally follows that your reactions to what is happening are going to be out of the ordinary, too. No one wants to pay fifteen or even five bucks to see the everyday; you can get that right around your street or in your home or on TV. What we want to see at an audition is the real you reacting to a remarkable situation in a remarkable and unique way. There's only one person like you in the entire world. Trust yourself to use *that* with truth and imagination.

I have found that in most circumstances actors use "character" as a limitation. I ask, "Why wouldn't you fall in love with him?" and the actress replies, "It isn't possible. My character would never fall in love with a man like that."

It happens so often that now I know it to be a fact that for most actors characterization means chiefly what their characters *won't* do. As soon as an actor puts such a limitation on his work, he's being *less* than himself, imprisoned in a straitjacket of dont's. With so little freedom to feel, how can an actor give a good audition? Put aside the limitations that instant characterizations inevitably instill; allow anything to be possible; make choices that give you the *maximum* possible involvement. If there's a possibility, however unlikely, however remote, that you might love the other character in the scene, say yes to the possibility. There's more feeling in potential love than there is in the impossibility of it. Feeling is what an actor is looking for; why not pick the most?

"What are you doing with the other character in your scene?" I ask an actor. He tells me, "I don't want to be with her; I want to get away from her." I ask him, "Then why don't you go? Just get up and walk away. We're all free to." Half the readings I see are about people who wish they weren't there. Who wants to see all that reluctance? Who wants to spend time with people who wish they were somewhere else? I want to see an actor who has found a reason for being there and a relationship that makes him *want* to confront the other character.

That's what this book is about: finding a reason for being there on that stage, finding a reason to express your fullest feelings deeply and importantly, saying yes to the possibilities that are within a relationship. Human beings, fortunately, don't operate out of reason (for if they did, no one would become an actor). What motivates human beings are their dreams. Dreams of love, dreams of fulfillment, dreams of success, dreams of beauty and power. It's what we wish would happen that makes us do everything we do.

This book is about finding the dream in you and learning to put it right up there on the stage, where everybody can see.

You have to be crazy, thank God, to want to do that.

1

Practical Aspects of the Audition

Let us consider some practical aspects of the reading situation first. There are two important *physical* aspects of readings that actors tend to forget: being seen and being heard.

Being seen is a problem because the unions allow only a single-bulb work light to be used for auditions. (It costs hundreds to have proper lights for auditions, so actors should complain to the stagehands' and lighting technicians' unions, not to the poor producers.) All of the creative people involved in the audition situation suffer. If you the actor think it's tough to go out there on that dark stage and do a reading in a limited area where there may be some feeble light, consider the plight of the auditors: they have to sit there for hours peering through the dusk trying to figure out what the actors look like who are auditioning for them. Since the light is so severely limited, it's important for the actor *to be in it*—not three feet to the left of it or upstage of it. Therefore I suggest the actor ask one of the two questions I consider it legitimate for an actor to ask at a reading: "Am I in the light?" Auditors will always be happy to tell you just exactly where the light is because it's a lot easier for them to be able to see you rather than search for you in darkness. But be sure to *listen to the answer* and then check again to make sure you have put yourself in the light. I find half the actors whom I instruct as to the location of our meagre light don't hear what I've said, since they go into darkness instead of into light.

(One of the reasons auditors are so reluctant to answer any questions put to them by actors is that so few of the actors seem, by their subsequent actions, to have listened to the answers. I suppose in the overwhelming nervousness of the audition situation it is hard for an actor to absorb the information given to him, but I suggest that one good way out of the generalized nervousness is for him *to listen* to what is being said.)

Remember also that frequently the light source is almost directly overhead, so putting your feet in the pool of light you see on the floor is not going to be a guarantee that your face will be seen. Ask: Can I be seen? Better still, practice at home with a *high* overhead light and learn to judge from seeing the pool of light on the floor about where you should stand so your face can be seen from out front.

You must also be heard. I hazard that 64 percent of the actors who audition for the stage cannot be heard. Directors are forever asking me, "But will we be able to hear her?" Perhaps this comes from this era of television and the syndrome of the Whispering Ingenue, whose husky whispers are supposed to be sexy (Lord help us for what Marilyn Monroe inflicted on the young actresses of America), although we find that just as many young men cannot be heard. Particular attention should be paid to a fact: virtually no actor is too loud, but over half of them are too soft to be heard comfortably.

Keep in mind that you rehearse in your apartment. Can you take just that onto the stage of a big theatre? Realize the kind of greater amplification you will need. In the years of teaching I have found an interesting thing: I no longer work on amplification in 98 percent of the actors or make any effort to get them to speak louder because if an actor truly desires to communicate his feelings to the other person on stage with him, he will be heard. My not hearing is due to the actor not communicating. If I work on getting the actor to communicate, strongly, urgently, he can then usually be heard.

The 2 percent who are exceptions to this? I find there are a few people who prefer not to be heard, who do not want to communicate at all. Perhaps they get more attention through the protests of their would-be listeners than they would if they had been heard. Give that a good long thought if you're one of those actors who consistently cannot be heard.

But for the 98 percent majority, you will be heard if you want to be. And that depends on the depth of your need to communicate what you think and feel to the other person on stage with you.

Earlier I said there are two legitimate questions an actor may ask at an audition. I mentioned one—that you not only may but should ask if you are in the light—and here is the other:

If you are asked to read "cold"—without having seen the script in advance—always ask if you might have time to go offstage to look it over. In the majority of cases, you will be given time to go off for a look.

However, if the auditors say, "No, why don't you just read it now?" then do say, "Without even reading it over?" to which they will be forced to reply, "Yes." And then you give them your gamest, most plucky smile and bravely sail into unknown, unchartered, untoward territory. By your question you will make it very clear that you haven't the foggiest, which will in turn have to be taken into account by them. In addition you've expressed your willingness to do whatever they want, however foolhardy.

If you don't ask for time to look it over, of course most auditors will let you stand right there and hang yourself. Do ask for time; 90 percent of the time you'll get it. But if you don't get time, don't pout; be very brave.

Who Conducts the Audition?

You may read for anyone from one person to ten or fifteen people. Usually there is the director and/or the casting director, since in most cases it is the director who is the most important vote in deciding who is cast in a show. The producer also frequently has an important voice in casting. In Broadway shows, the playwright is an important auditor, since it states in his contract that he has approval of the cast. In addition, if it is a musical, there is the musical director, the choreographer, the lyricist, the composer, the book writer, and their various assistants. The production stage manager frequently has a voice in casting. In television there are network producers and sponsors and a host of others who may voice their views on the casting. Whether it's one person watching your audition or thirty, you give it your all every time—and no matter how often you have to read for the same part.

I've had actors refuse to come in to read for a role they've read for several times before. I think this is foolish. You wouldn't be called back if there wasn't interest in you. What's the difference if you read for twelve different roles or for one role twelve times? Either way it's twelve cracks at getting a job. Sometimes on that thirteenth reading you do get the role.

Shall I Ask Who the Auditors Are?

Please don't. Ever. If the auditors wanted you to know who they are, they would introduce themselves. Frequently they don't want you to know who they are, preferring to conduct the auditions in as much anonymity as they can achieve. Sometimes they are perfectly willing for you to know who they are, but they don't want to go through the process of introductions forty times a day. It can get very wearing for the auditors, who prefer to spend that valuable time finding out who *you* are.

There are actresses (oddly enough, actors rarely do it) who turn to the auditors with a big Howard Johnson hostess smile and say, "Whom am I auditioning for?" thus forcing the auditors to introduce themselves, which often results in resentment against the actress who put them in this uncomfortable position and wasted their valuable time and energy.

You're better off not knowing whom you audition for, anyhow. It's just one more piece of information to make you more nervous, information that gets in your way.

How Do You Find Out What the Auditors Want?

You can't. You shouldn't. It's a total waste of your time to try to find out what the auditors want. What the auditors want is someone very interesting and talented in each and every role. That's all you should concern yourself with.

I think actors, particularly in New York, waste half their lives running around trying to find out "what they want." They get a half-baked rumor or a piece of information that only misleads them into trying to be "that" instead of being themselves in the role. And "that" may force them to change their hair color or have a nose operation or cut off a leg or wear sixteen-inch heels or walk on their knees —little of which is of value in the audition situation.

Remember, as I keep telling the auditors, all they can choose from is what exists. They may have Someone Glorious in mind, but that has to be eventually translated into the reality of a living, breathing human actor. It will probably be far from what the creators had in mind when they started out. It could be you.

When I worked on the film of THE GRADUATE, director Mike Nichols told me to find a new young James Stewart, tall, basketball player, Eastern Ivy League college-type fellow. I was sent to Princeton and Yale and Harvard to find an unknown. College jocks and college actors came into New York from all over the country to be interviewed. The search went on for months. Who got the role? Short, non-Ivy League,non-basketball-playing Dustin Hoffman.

And how did Dustin Hoffman get the role? By auditioning for a part in a Broadway musical he didn't get. When I was casting the musical THE APPLE TREE, for Mike Nichols and producer Stuart Ostrow, I tried to persuade Dustin Hoffman (then an unknown actor, having done two Ronald Ribman plays Off Broadway) to come in to audition for the lead role that Alan Alda eventually got. Dustin told me he'd only had six singing lessons, so I said, "Go take two more and come in to audition." Every day we had auditions, I would put

Dustin Hoffman down on my list, and each day he failed to appear (because he was frightened of doing a singing audition.) It got to be a running gag that Mike Nichols would ask me, "Is the famous Dustin Hoffman coming in today?" After weeks of persuasion, the unknown Dustin Hoffman did come in to audition. He was right: he couldn't sing. However, he gave a marvelous reading of such imagination, intelligence, and humor that Mike Nichols never forgot it. The producer of THE GRADUATE later told me he nearly went into a state of catatonic shock because he couldn't believe Dustin Hoffman was Mr. Nichols's choice for the Ivy Leaguer. It made a star out of Dustin Hoffman.

The moral is: (1) Always go to audition for everything, if they allow you, even if you think you're wrong for it. And (2) Whomever the auditors *say* they're looking for can change into someone totally opposite. The actor who is talented and interesting and committed is more likely to get the role than someone who is "right."

The mistakes of casting usually come about because the auditors cast someone who looked "right" rather than someone who was more talented but different from their image.

What Do the Auditors Expect from a Reading?

An opening night performance. That's all.

Directors and producers will deny this, of course. And they are right to do so, since what they should be looking for is the opportunity to explore who you are and what you can bring to the role. On a Bob Fosse show, for example, the show we start out with on paper is never the show we end up with because Mr. Fosse uses the rehearsal and out-of-town tryouts to tailor the show to fit the talents of the people he has hired to be in it. (Which is one reason a Fosse show is so difficult to recast—the other being that so few performers can fulfill the particular dance requirements of a Fosse show.)

What the auditors do need from a reading is a full experience of who you are and what you can do. An actor *can* achieve in a reading the same free use of himself that he uses in a performance. It's all in knowing how to use yourself fully, in employing your imagination, in being willing to take risks.

It doesn't matter what the auditors *say* they want; your job as an actor is to show them who you are and how sensitive you are to the feelings in the role.

Why Is It I Can Act It Well When I'm Doing a Play But Can't Do That in a Reading?

You can do in a reading what you do in a performance. It's a matter of learning how to use yourself and to *ask the right questions*. A fascinating fact I find in my work: if I ask the questions, the actors can usually come up with the answers. Clearly that means the actor must learn to ask the right questions of himself.

The twelve guideposts that follow this chapter will give you the right questions to ask. Putting the answers into your reading will give you a good audition.

The major reason I started teaching actors how to audition is because in my work as a casting director I would see an actor perform in a play Off Broadway or Off-Off in a church or a basement theatre or at ELT, and on the basis of what I saw him perform, I would ask him to come in for a Broadway show or a film I was casting. But he would not show the ability I had seen when he had performed. So I realized the actor didn't know how to audition, since he couldn't do in the audition situation what he had done in performing. You can.

Why Do You Call the Audition Situation a War Between the Actors and the Auditors?

Actors feel as if they're going to the battlefront when they go to an audition. They seem to regard the auditors as "the enemy." If it is a war, then realize that the auditors have *all* the power on their side. An actor cannot win the war by hostility but only by wooing the enemy. Fighting them will only result in losing the battle.

You may well ask why an actor would express hostility at an audition. He doesn't intend to, probably, but his nervousness, his insecurity, his feeling that he is being put on the spot and judged and very likely rejected all combine to make him feel the auditors are out to get him. The tensions of the situation create a feeling of being unjustly treated, so the actor is likely to feel hostile—and all he needs is a trigger to set him off. Most of the directors and producers I have worked for do not intend to be rude or hurtful but sometimes the tensions on their side of the fence cause them to be abrupt. It would be helpful if actors would remember that the directors and producers are afraid of the actors: It stands to reason, doesn't it, since their professional life is in your hands. With so much fear on both sides, an occasional expression of hostility is bound to happen, but it is always to the disadvantage of the actor. I counsel all actors: Control your hostility. I have seen actors lose good roles that might have importantly furthered their careers because of a mistaken display of hostility or temper. You may get temporary relief about a situation you feel, perhaps rightly, is unjust, but it ain't worth it. You lose.

Casting a Broadway comedy for one of Broadway's most successful directors, Joshua Logan, who is also one of the world's kindest, we were looking for a new leading man to play opposite our star lady. Through the weeks of auditions we found several prospects—some names, some relatively new—but one totally unknown actor was our chief candidate. Josh wanted the newcomer to have every chance, so on the day of the final readings (set up for the approval of the star and the producer), he arranged the order of the readings so our candidate would come on two thirds of the way through: late enough so the star would have others less impressive to compare him with, but not so late that she would be tired and weary of it all. Those final readings are always testy, since the whole project is riding on what happens. The air crackles with nervous tension.

Let us call our unknown actor Candidate A, the one Josh and I thought was an exciting discovery. For Candidate A to appear in the lead role opposite an important star could mean a whole career ahead of him—if he was good, if the play succeeded, and all those other ifs that make up show biz. Worse luck, our Candidate A got an audition for a commercial the very day of our finals. He came early to the readings, explained his predicament to the stage manager, who sympathetically ushered him right onstage to read first. The director was deep in a discussion with the star about *her* views on how the leading man was to be cast when he looked up and saw his candidate on stage reading away. "Oh, no, no, no," he said, "there's been a terrible mistake! Could Candidate A please wait in the wings?" Since there were other actors waiting backstage, no one could explain to Candidate A why he was asked to return later. Off he went to try to get his commercial audition over with first. He came back on a break in between readings for the commercial and said he had to read for us at once. Once again he was ushered onstage, just at the point when the producer was having a heated disagreement with the star and the author, with Mr. Logan doing his best to referee. If Candidate A had read then, no one would have noticed. Once again the director had to say, "No, I'm sorry, not yet, please!" and motion the bewildered actor offstage. Finally, an hour later, the timing seemed at last to be right. Mr. Logan asked for Candidate A, who had been stewing in the wings, certain he would lose his commercial and this role. Candidate A came onstage, looking very hostile, started to read, threw down his script, and yelled, "I can't read this damn thing! I've never been treated so miserably in my life! Take your damn play and shove it!" And then he marched out of the theatre.

Mr. Logan was dumbfounded. All he knew was that he'd tried to protect Candidate A all day, to give him the best possible chance and circumstance and time, and now he was repaid for it by the rudest conduct he had ever experienced from an actor at an audition. None of us out front knew the backstage circumstances until much later—too late to mitigate. The actor did not get that job, needless to say. Since the theatre is a small world, word got around of this actor's display of temperament, which hurt his career for a long time. Not justly, perhaps, but the actor didn't handle a ticklish, trying situation with tack or diplomacy.

The moral: When you think they're dumping on you, they just may be trying to help you.

Hold your anger until you get home; it's never going to do you any good to let it out at an audition. Go home and throw supper out the window or beat up your mother or throw a knife at your wife, but how can you expect to win if you yell at the auditors? They got all the power; you got none.

It's a difficult situation, for the auditors have to reject so many people so often. For the actors, each failure to get a job seems like a personal rejection.

The actor's demeanor before and after the actual reading is usually the only opportunity he has to convey what sort of person he is. This is the time when the auditors are very sensitive indeed to the slightest indications of reluctance, resentment, and antagonism, so the actor would do well to cover up such feelings, if he has them, with a strong action to extend extreme goodwill toward the auditors. Directors frequently ask me, "What do you know about him? Is he easy to work with? Does he take direction?" It is important that the actor convey to the auditors that the answer to all these questions is a big *yes:* "I am easy to work with, I am affable and rational, I take direction well, I am imaginative and cooperative, I don't pout or become hostile."

The producers and directors have enough temperament from the star of a show. They don't want any from you.

The easiest way to convey your conviviality and amiability is to make a game of it. Remember what the stakes are, so make the game a sincere one; no one likes to play any game with an insincere player. Most of you go into an audition situation closed up, in order to protect yourself. Learn to open yourself up, so that you can *receive* the experience. It constantly amazes me to see what an advantageous effect an open actor can have on the auditors. They are looking for actors they can like; they can't like you if you are hidden from them self-protectively. Express a willingness to like them so they can like you. They want to.

Why Do the Auditors Eat Sandwiches and Drink Coffee During My Audition?

They eat or drink coffee during everyone's audition. Evidently auditors don't eat in the outside world. They're at an audition for half an hour, and they call out for something to eat. Don't think it's personally directed toward *your* audition, for the auditors are nervous through everyone's.

Don't be concerned if you notice the auditors are under the seats of the theatre. They spend a good deal of time down there, looking for pencils they have dropped, cigarette lighters, and matches. And when they drop their containers of coffee, they are busy down there on their hands and knees mopping up since the house manager frowns upon anything spilled on the floor of the theatre.

How Do I Conduct My Exit and Entrance?

This is your chance to show both how businesslike and how charming and open you are. Most actors are busy dealing with the agony they are undergoing rather then trying to communicate to the auditors that they are pleasant and outgoing human beings.

What Do I Do When They Ask Me "What Have You Done?"

This is your biggest chance to express who you are rather than merely what you have done. You should prepare this response as if it were a personal one-act play created especially about you. A mere recitation of facts isn't going to do you any good. You should combine with the factual information your humor, your charm, and your personality.

Work on this one-act play. Write it, get direction, rehearse it. Have it ready to perform every time you are asked. There are times when your presentation of what you have done is as important as the reading you give.

What If I Have an Insignificant Résumé with Little Experience?

What you have actually done is not as important as how you present it. I've heard Broadway actors reply when asked what they have done, "I've only done five Broadway shows and three running parts on soap operas, two films and some TV." That is a lot of experience made to seem like none at all. It's up to you to take pride in what you have done, to make it sound important and worthwhile. If you don't think so, the auditors never will.

No matter how little you've done, most of you have done something. You have studied, you have acted, somewhere. Present it with pride. Make something of it. Don't believe the auditors when they disesteem your experience; believe in your own worth.

Everyone has to begin somewhere. Barbra Streisand had only appeared in two brief engagements in Village nightclubs when she auditioned for the role of Miss Marmelstein in I CAN GET IT FOR YOU WHOLESALE. After she sang, when they asked her for her experience, she didn't tell them how little she had done. She did an improvisation that was a brilliant exploration of what she could do. She took a colorful risk: it paid off.

I had seen her sing in a Village club and asked her to do a theatre audition, since many club singers can't be heard in a theatre. She came onstage in an oversize raccoon coat and looked around, way up to the balcony. "I got to fill this big place?" she asked. Then she sang, and she did fill it up. She dropped her raccoon on the floor for her second number, saying, "I like it here," and then she went into that slow version of "Happy Days Are Here Again" for which she later became famous. That was a lady who knew how to audition, but I suspect her preparation was extensive and very little was left to chance.

Most important was the communication, all through her audition, that she liked being there, belonged being there, wanted to be heard, wanted to be seen, wanted response.

What Do I Do If I'm Late for an Audition?

Inquire of the stage manager or the secretary if the auditors have inquired about you or noticed that you are late. If no one has been inconvenienced by your being late, say nothing about it.

But if you have inconvenienced the auditors and an explanation of your tardiness is necessary, then say to them: "I'm sorry I was late. I was held up at another audition." This is one of the few untruths I advocate for actors, because (1) it saves other long-winded explanations about your health and the public transportation system that are of no interest to the auditors, (2) it's an excuse perfectly understandable and acceptable to the auditors, since they so often are forced to keep actors waiting, and (3) it indicates your desirability because someone else wanted you to read for them as well.

About your health: It is best to learn at the outset that your health is of no interest to anyone else on this earth, except perhaps to your beloveds, and to them only because it enables them to burden you with tales about *their* health. Strangers are never interested in your health and don't want to hear about it. If you arrive on crutches and in a cast, carry it off lightly by saying it'll all be off by the time rehearsals start. Don't burden the auditors with your other difficulties, either, such as being held up in crosstown traffic or the breakdown of the subway or having to take your ailing pets to the vet.

After telling your little white lie about being held up at another audition, should they ask for what, explain that you are superstitious and would rather not mention what it is. The auditors are superstitious, too; they'll understand and probe no further.

Should I Memorize the Script?

Never. It's a waste of time.

It's called a reading, so do a reading. Don't waste your valuable time memorizing a script, when that time can much more valuably be spent in exploring the guideposts. Except in rare instances, no one expects you to have learned the script. On the contrary, for you to appear onstage without your script might cause the auditors to judge your audition in terms of performance rather than reading: you're not ready for that. No matter how easily you memorize, the chances are great that you'll forget a line, or that your concentration will be spent remembering lines instead of dealing with the really important considerations of a reading.

Learn to regard those pieces of paper as your friend and ally. They state: "This is a reading I'm doing, not a performance." Welcome the script instead of trying to get rid of it. Once you accept it, it's useful to you rather than a hinderance. I hear actors say repeatedly, "Oh, if only I didn't have this script!" But you haven't had rehearsal time, you haven't worked with a director or your fellow actor, so you *need* the paper. There's more freedom in learning to work with the script than all those efforts to get rid of it.

There are some rare actors who memorize so easily that a read or two through the script has it learned. To them, I advise: Take the script with you. Pretend to refer to it even if you don't need it. You'll find more often than not you will need it, so have it there, handy at all times. A performance takes a lot of rehearsal time; a reading can be done in short order if you've learned how to use yourself with the specifics of the twelve guideposts to tell you where to focus.

Memorized readings come out like canned music. Memorization tends to lead to line readings, which cuts down on communication. *A reading should be more akin to an improvisation than a finished performance.* Everything in a reading should be happening for the first time.

What If the Director Directs Me at a Reading?

Listen to him. Be sure you understand what he is saying to you. Then translate what he has said into the terms of the preparation you have done and *add* what he has said to your audition.

Always remember: *Add* to what you have done. I have seen most actors *change* their reading because of directions given to them; then they lose the job. The director shakes his head, "Too bad. Can't take direction." Even if the director asks you to *change* your reading, what he means is *add* what he says to what you have been doing. He does not mean throw away everything you were doing, or he wouldn't have spoken to you, singled you out, and given you direction in the first place.

How Do I Judge My Reading? How Do I Find Out Why I Wasn't Accepted?

There is no value in finding out why you weren't accepted; you'll rarely learn the truth, anyhow. Since all the considerations in casting are relative, what good will it do for you to find out you're too short for the leading lady or too tall for the leading man? The solution would be to go home and cut your leg off or put on a pair of stilts; neither will help you. Casting is a very subjective process for the auditors, naturally, no matter what objective criteria they use. Given readings of equal excellence, they are more than likely to decide because "I like her." There's nothing you can do about that, so it's better not to concern yourself with it. The reasons for not choosing you are likely to be myriad and complex, from the fact that you look too like another actor already cast to their subjective reaction of not liking your looks or the timbre of your voice to the fact that you remind them of their first wife—reasons you can do nothing to control or alter.

As for judging your own reading, judge it not on the basis of whether or not you fulfilled what you think they wanted but on the basis of how fully you were able to express your own emotional life in terms of the character and situation. In the ensuing chapters twelve guideposts are discussed: use *them* as the judgments of your own readings.

How Do I Get a Reading?

The best way is through an agent.

There are other, more hazardous ways, such as sending your picture to a producer or a director or a casting director, followed up by imaginative letters to interest them in you. Many actors "make the rounds" of production offices, pestering the people there into giving them a reading. Sometimes this system works, if you've got a lot of shoes and a thick skin that doesn't mind rejections in person. I think the same thing can be accomplished by the mails, making it a more pleasant process on both sides. The energy you use trying to break into a production office would be better applied to getting yourself an agent.

Once you get an agent, you can't sit back and wait for him to phone you. An actor must still read the trade papers and keep abreast of what's going on so he can prod his agent into getting him appointments for projects for which he might be suitable.

Being an actor takes twenty-four hours of each day, and over half of that is spent in trying to get a job rather than in performing it.

Should Actors Go to an Open Call?

In the Broadway theatre, the actors' union (Actors Equity Association) requires each production to conduct what is called an open call, conducted by the producer so that any member of Equity may be seen for the play. Actors complain to me frequently that they go to be seen for roles that are already cast. True. Don't complain to the producers, complain to Equity; the producers are merely complying with Equity rules. These rules are made in good faith to give Equity members a wider chance to be considered, but it sometimes results in waste of time and energy. Most of the time spent going to open calls will result in nothing of value to the actor except the chance to be with other actors and to hear the latest gossip and complaints.

However, students of mine have gotten jobs at an open call, so it can be worthwhile. As with every ratio in this business of being in the theatre, the chances are few.

What Will My Agent Do for Me?

Not much.

Agents can get you appointments for readings. Not always, but often. They negotiate your contract (and sometimes nearly negotiate you right out of the job). But they can never get you a job.

Agents are wheeler-dealers. I think it is fairly safe to say, after twenty years of dealing with them, that most agents are fairly uncaring and insensitive to the actor. Their goal is money and power, being the business middlemen in a creative world, although some of them do have a penchant for mothering. But one could not be an agent if one were too sensitive, so look elsewhere for love, caring, or loyalty.

An agent is good if you're in demand and no good if you're not.

An agent is necessary. An actor cannot thrive in the business of theatre or film or TV without one.

Is the Stage Manager the Actor's Friend?

Stage managers are often sympathetic to the plight of the actor, but it is good to remember they are members of the enemy camp. If you cause a scene backstage, count on the stage manager reporting it to the producer, director and other auditors. You've got to be charming and pleasant everywhere around a theatre, offstage as well as on. Save your fits for home.

What Should I Audition For? What If It's for a Role I'm Not Right For?

I think an actor should audition every damn chance he gets. If you're twenty-three and blond and you get a chance to audition for an eighty-year-old brunette grandmother, go and audition. If the part requires someone six foot three and you're five foot two and they'll let you, read for it. Read for Off-Off-Broadway, read for Off Broadway, read for ELT, read for stock, read for community theatre, read for anything where anyone will allow you to read. You need the practice.

Don't decide in advance you don't want a role. Actors don't know what is right for them. I've had to persuade many an actor to come in to read for a role he thought he "wasn't right for," and after the reading the actor sees the role and himself in it in a different light. At least give yourself the added information you get from doing a reading. Then if you are absolutely sure you can't do the role (and you're probably wrong if you're worth your salt as an actor), then turn it down for the only other untruth I advocate for actors: Tell them you were offered another job for which you had previously read. I suggest this out of politeness because you hurt their feelings if you tell them you don't like the role or the script. They don't like being rejected any more than you do, so do it nicely.

Why Do You Advocate A Mail Rather Than an In-Person Campaign?

Because a mail campaign can create in the auditors or the agent a desire to see you. If they want to see you, you're in a much stronger position than forcing them because you want to see them.

Because mail can be opened and read at the convenience of the auditor, whereas your drop-in visit or phone call can occur at a highly inconvenient and unwanted time. In my own work, for example, I don't have time during the day to deal with actors, since I'm dealing with agents and the producer and the director, setting up auditions and being at auditions. At night, when the phone stops, I am free to read any mail you send me. I can be in a receptive mood then; if you catch me during the day, I resent the time you're robbing from me that has been allocated elsewhere.

Because it's easier to be rejected by mail than in person.

Because you can keep up a mail campaign indefinitely, getting more and more imaginative as you do. Enough in-person visits or phone calls and they get to loathe the sight of your face and the sound of your voice. I sent David Merrick a letter a week for seven months before he called me in to see him. I never complained in any of those letters; I wrote about his work and my interest in it and reactions to it. Finally he saw me. I got the job I wanted that way.

Because it's a more considerate way to woo the auditors.

Because it always gives you time to think before you speak.

This is merely my view. If you want to beard lions in their dens, go right ahead. Prepare to be bitten.

What Do I Do at an Interview?

Most actors come into the interview situation wearing a thick mask, spending their energies to protect themselves. It's rough interviewing someone who is determined to keep himself hidden. It's a lot harder to interview people than it is to be interviewed. If you would keep *that* in mind—the rough job the interviewer has—you might be able to relax a bit more and be more helpful. Try a little empathy. Put yourself in the interviewer's shoes. Help the interviewer. He needs help!

Try to give. Try to open up. Try to see who the interviewer is. I've had many occasions to interview actors all day—thirty, forty of them—and then go on the street at lunch or at the end of the day and run into the same actors. I say hello and they look blankly at me, as if I were a mugger. I remember them, and they never saw me. I've interviewed thirty people, and they've had *one* interview, and they don't know what the guy who interviewed them looks like.

Talk about something other than your résumé and what the interview is for. Be sensitive to the reactions of the interviewer; if what you're saying bores him, choose something else. Garson Kanin is the best interviewer I've ever watched. He gets people to open up and reveal themselves because he's really curious about every human being that crosses his door, so he really talks to them: about cooking, baseball, do they sew? what do they think about being married or having children? do they like being single? anything that comes into his head that interests him and them. He doesn't concern himself in the interview so much with what you've done as with who you are and how you feel about stuff, so he talks to you about stuff instead of your résumé. The résumé he can always read later.

Bob Fosse is another who gives the actor a great chance in the interview because he creates a relationship between peers, not between king and subject. He gives of himself so that the actor has a chance to give back. Most of you sit there with your dukes up, this look on your face as if you expected to be hit. Yes, I know, you all tell me how mean the interviewer is. I think that's because you have so little sympathy for that poor soul. You ask to be hit, so he hits you.

I watch actors when they come out of a Kanin or Fosse interview. They're surprised, they're beaming, they say, "He was so *nice.*" By which they mean he was interested. Why don't you try being interested in the interviewer? It would sure help break the ice.

Reveal yourself. Talk. Take a chance. What have you got to lose? You'll lose out on the interview anyhow if you sit there like a mummy. Better to take the chance of communicating to the person sitting on the other side of that desk. Treat him like a prospective friend instead of a hangman. It might work.

What to Wear for an Audition?

Wear what is appropriate.

If you're auditioning for T. S. Eliot's THE COCKTAIL PARTY, don't come in blue jeans. And if you're auditioning for THE INDIAN WANTS THE BRONX, don't come in your tuxedo.

When I was casting the musical version of PICNIC, we flew an actor all that expensive way from California especially to audition for the role of Hal. He came wearing a spiffy black silk suit elegant enough for Sky Masterson in GUYS AND DOLLS. Nothing could have been more wrong for the role of Hal. It's hard enough for the poor auditors to judge your rightness for roles—do you have to make it doubly difficult? When we asked him to take off his jacket and roll up his sleeves so we could get a better idea of Hal, he refused: "I just paid three hundred dollars for this suit and I'm wearing it." We had just paid his fare from California; we deserved a better throw of the dice than he was willing to give us.

I do not suggest you wear costumes; I suggest you dress appropriately if you know what the role is. If you don't, then wear something unobtrusive, so they can see *you* rather than what you're wearing.

Always wear to the second audition (and any subsequent auditions, no matter how many) the same thing you wore to the first audition. The reason? Because auditors frequently make mental (or written) notes of what you are wearing to help them identify you. If you change costumes, they frequently get confused. Jerry Robbins asked me at the end of a day of auditions why I hadn't brought back the girl in the orange sweater. I had, but she was wearing a purple dress. I'm not sure we ever did get that straightened out. You can help the auditors by wearing the same thing every time you audition.

Why Do We Have to Go Through the Torture of Auditions?

Because no one has ever devised a better way to cast. If you think of one, let us know.

Even if the auditors know an actor, even if they have worked with an actor before, it gives everyone a much better chance to find out *if* the actor reads for the role. It's not a surefire method, of course, how could anything so subjective be certain? It's long and it's difficult and it's very expensive and in many ways it's a lot harder on the auditors than it is on the actors, but it's the only way we've got.

It's possible for an actor to get himself into such a healthy frame of mind that he enjoys auditioning. It gives him a chance to try on the role, to show his stuff, to practice his craft, to give himself a high, to experiment and take a risk, to meet a challenge the way a mountain climber views a new mountain.

The guideposts that follow may help you to do that.

2

The Twelve Guideposts

Guidepost 1: Relationship

Creating relationship is the heart of acting. It is basic. It is essential.

Start with the question: What is my relationship to this other character in the scene I am about to do? Facts are never enough, although they will help you begin. Determine if you are the son and she is the mother, if you are the lover and she is your beloved, if you are the husband and she the wife. Once you know *the fact* of a relationship, you are ready to explore how you *feel* about this other character—since a mere fact doesn't give you any feeling to work with, does it? Many actors tend to settle for fact: I am her son, I am her husband. That really tells you nothing you can work with as an actor. You must go further, into the realm of the emotions.

You need to ask feeling questions about your emotional attitude toward the other character: Do you love him? Do you hate him? Do you resent him? How much? Do you want to help him? Do you want to get in his way? What do you want from him? What do you want him to give you? These are the most important questions to ask. The answers to them will allow you to function emotionally in the scene. That is your goal.

Often actors are not given the entire script but only a scene or a section of a scene, from which it is frequently difficult to determine the fact of the relationship. It may not tell you whether the other character is your brother or your husband. That's not important— even though you must make a choice, of course. But it's not important if you're right or wrong: what is important is your commitment to whatever feeling you choose. Fact alone never helps you, only emotional attitude does. What good is it to know the other character is your brother if you don't decide how you feel toward him in this scene? Consider your brother: there have been times when you have felt loving and sweet toward him, other times when he so enraged you that you could have killed him. And there were times when both these reactions occurred in the same scene!

Frequently I will ask an actress after she has read a scene: "What is the relationship?" and she will answer, "He's my husband." "So?" I ask.

She looks consternated. "He's my husband" is as far as she's taken it. It's not far enough. The fact that you are married to a man tells nothing about how you feel toward him at this moment in this scene. That is what you need to explore. That is why the *fact* of a relationship is of no value to the actor unless it leads him to explore the *feeling* in the relationship *now*. Not how it was when you got married, not how it was last week when he got a raise (although all this information is of value in creating an emotional past to the relationship), but how you feel now. The *now* is the imperative question you must answer.

EXAMPLE

THE MIDDLE OF THE NIGHT *by* PADDY CHEYEVSKY

Take the scene between the young wife and husband. She married a sexy, good-looking stud and their sex life has been great, but she has found the relationship superficial and unrewarding on other levels. The husband goes off on a job in Las Vegas, and the wife meets and falls in love with a much older man, with whom she has great tenderness and communication such as she has never before experienced. She writes to her husband to tell him she wants a divorce in order to marry the older man. The husband returns to find out why she would possibly reject him for a man old enough to be her father, and to get her back. The wife is torn between her sexual attraction for her husband and her desire for a better life with the older man. Almost every actress who reads for this scene leaves out the sexual attraction for the husband and instead regards the end of their marriage as a *fait accompli*: I am through with this marriage; leave me alone; I am not interested in you; I am going to marry another, older, wiser, nicer man. That is what the words say. But when the actress leaves out the attraction on a sexual level that still exists for her husband, when she does not use the feeling she had for him and that he can still arouse in her, then the scene is flat, cold, unemotional. There is no conflict, there is no humanity, the scene does not touch us.

The playwright does not provide the words for the actress to know this because the character never *says*, "I am still attracted to you, even though I want to be free of you." Instead she uses words of rejection almost entirely in order to protect herself from letting this attraction show. Should she give in to this attraction, she will be lost once again in this shallow relationship, so she fights against it with *words* intended to cover over the emotions she is feeling. Of course, the scene can be read as a scene of pure rejection and hatred; most actresses do it that way. But it doesn't work.

If you were to ask that character if she is still sexually interested in her husband, she probably would say, "No! I am not." That is why the actress needs to know more than the character knows.

How do you find this out? By putting yourself, a young and attractive girl, in the position of the character. Have a husband who is very sexy, with whom you've had a great time in bed every time; contrast him with an older man, who is a father figure to you, with whom you have never been to bed but whom you respect and feel close and warm with, to whom you can talk as you've never managed to talk to your husband. Put these two feelings into the scene: Create the conflict between a *desire* for your husband, a wish you could be in bed with him right now, and your determination to have a higher-level, more meaningful relationship with the older man. Create the *feelings* as *you* would feel them, not as you think the character would (that can lead you far astray from your own emotional life, which is what you will have to use in the scene no matter how much you study and analyze *her*).

This scene from THE MIDDLE OF THE NIGHT explains why I say every scene is a love scene. The actor should ask the question, "Where is the love?" of every scene, or he won't find the deepest emotional content. This does not mean that every scene is about Romeo and Juliet–type love; sometimes the scene is about the absence or the deprivation of love. But by asking "Where is the love?" you come up with an answer that will involve you emotionally with more immediacy than if you fail to ask that question. As an actor you should always be looking for the most immediate emotional involvement: What will involve you right now, not tomorrow or next week.

I ask questions of the actress and actor who have just auditioned this scene from THE MIDDLE OF THE NIGHT:

MS   Where is the love in this scene?

GIRL   I don't love my husband anymore. I love the older man. No, I'm not sure I love the older man: I have grave doubts about it. I would *like* to love him, but I don't think I do.

MS   So there is no love in the scene?

GIRL   Not really.

MS   Doesn't give you much to work with. Say yes to every question about love in the scene—and then tell me.

GIRL   You mean, yes I love my husband and yes I do love the older man? I love both of them?

MS   Isn't that a more vivid choice? Doesn't it create conflict in you, and isn't conflict what an actor is seeking in the audition? To have something strong to work with. Of course always say yes to the question of love. It gives you a rich emotional involvement. What does saying no give you to work with in a scene?

GIRL   How can I be in love with two men at the same time?

MS   Today you've made a discovery. People can be in love with two people at the same time. Perhaps each one thinks as you do: This can't happen, I cannot be in love with two men at the same time. But it does happen

GIRL   Doesn't that make me fickle, shallow?

MS   Not unless you decide it does. I would never decide that. I'd decide it made me very needful of love, of having to make the right choice, of being torn between the two and wanting a choice that would make me happy.

GIRL   Do I love them both the same way?

MS   No. Of course not. Tell me the difference.

GIRL   I love the older man because he is kind and considerate, gentle, I can talk to him. I respect him. But I love my husband because he's young and sexy and kind of exciting, I guess.

MS   Don't guess. Say yes.

GIRL   Yes, I find him very exciting in bed. But out of bed, we have nothing to talk to each other about, which is why the marriage is falling apart. Sex isn't enough.

MS   Good. There's conflict in relationship with your husband from the start, which gives you good material to work with.

GIRL   But on the other hand, I wonder if I can have any sex life with this older man. He's not really attractive, and he doesn't turn me on sexually. Can you make a marriage on respect and consideration when there's no excitement?

MS   Excellent.

GIRL   But what do I decide?

MS   That comes at the end of the play. Maybe a decision doesn't come into this scene. What is important is to make these questions *active* in the reading: keep asking the questions. Wanting to decide is more active than deciding.

GIRL   So I am trying to resolve this conflict in this scene with my husband, right? I'm trying to decide in favor of the sensible choice. I found out the sexual choice didn't work at all, so I want to choose the older man. I see! But I keep being attracted sexually to my young husband, which is why I keep saying "Go away" and "I'm going in the house" and yet I stay right there with him.

MS The *process* of trying to reach an emotional decision is always more dramatic than the achievement of it.

Then I ask some questions of the Young Husband:

MS Where is the love in the scene?

YOUNG HUSBAND From reading it I thought this was just an ego trip for this guy, that it hurt his pride to be losing his young attractive wife to an older guy. But after listening to you talk to her, I begin to see that if I choose that I love her, it'd be a lot deeper feeling to work with.

MS Right.

YH So I love her and I've come back to make sure I keep her.

MS Don't throw away your idea of the ego trip. Add that to being in love with her.

YH Ah. You mean, you can't compare me with an older man—of course I'm more desirable than he is.

MS Exactly.

YH And I think if I just get her into my arms, she'll give in. If I do that, then I can get her into the sack and I'll dazzle her and she'll forget all about that old man.

MS Very good choices. Now what's the conflict?

YH She wants to marry some one sensible, not like me at all.

MS Right. More.

YH More conflict? Oh. She's been unfaithful to me while I've been away working in Vegas. How can she do that to me?

MS Excellent. More.

YH I'm better in the sack than he'll ever be.

MS Fine. More.

YH Even though I want you back, don't think you're going to tie me down. I want to tie you down, you should be faithful to me, but I'm a man with a

roving eye so you can't expect me to be faithful
to you.

MS   Good choices. Now the scene has many levels of
relationship conflict for both of you.

Take any scene between the mother and the daughter in Shee-
lagh Delaney's A TASTE OF HONEY and it looks on the page like one
long fight, with the daughter resisting the mother on every turn. Ask
"Where is the love?" in this scene and most actresses tell me there
isn't any, so their rendition of the scene is all petulant, cold, withdrawn—and therefore not very attractive or interesting. Realize that
the daughter is yearning for love from the mother but never feels she
gets it yet keeps trying to get it. Then you have a scene that is active
and emotional for Jo instead of cold and detached. Realize that the
mother feels so guilty for not offering her daughter the love she
should have that she too keeps trying, although failing; she keeps
trying every visit to get her daughter on her side. Since the mother
is used to being liked by men, she should be liked by her daughter,
and she tries the same kind of wooing gamesmanship tactics on Jo.
Realize further that the mother is quite a charmer and very funny and
that Jo finds her very funny and quite a charmer, and you have a
scene that is warm and complex. Most actresses leave out the love
in A TASTE OF HONEY, so you get scenes of petulance and yelling,
on a single tiresome kitchen-drama level. Put in the love and it can
become funny and dear.

Take Chance Wayne and the Princess in SWEET BIRD OF YOUTH
by Tennessee Williams. Chance is clearly manipulating the Princess
in order to get to Hollywood and a chance to become a film star himself; she is using him for temporary expediency. Where is the love?
He wants her to love him because then she will be trapped into doing for him what he needs for a career in film. She wants him to love
her so she can be sure he'll be there when she needs and wants him.
Neither one is offering love, each one is demanding it of the other.
It's a rich love scene. Even though neither of them is anything but
narcissistic and selfish, it's love they want. Nothing less will get
them where they want to go.

I have been surprised to find that most actors (and therefore, I
suppose, most people) conceive of love as chiefly idealistic and al-
truistic. When I talk of Helen and Jo from TASTE OF HONEY or the
Princess and Chance in SWEET BIRD OF YOUTH, they say, "I
wouldn't call that love," because they don't find it admirable. Until
you expand your concept of what love is to include the various peculiar and perverse forms it can take in human relationships, you're go-

ing to have a hard time as an actor finding an emotional commitment to the scenes you're trying to act. The desire for love, to give it or receive it, and preferably both and simultaneously, is the chief pro-pellant in human beings. An actor had best learn that love comes in all forms, and in many more forms than only those he himself ad-mires.

An actor cannot act without creating a relationship with that other person who's onstage with him. Some actors do it instinctively; they are the lucky ones. But when the instincts don't work the way they should, the first thing an actor must do then is ask questions about the relationship and insist upon full emotional answers that can lead him to commit himself fully.

It's the full commitment that creates good acting. It's the achievement of a relationship of need and love that makes the audi-ence believe.

Guidepost 2: What Are You Fighting For? Conflict

It is customary for actors, I am told, to break a scene down into "beats," or sections, and then to find for each beat a motivation, or goal. Although I agree with this method, I find it does not go far enough. Many times when I ask an actor what his goal is in a scene, he will tell me, "I want to get away from this person. I want to run out of this room."

I then ask, "Why don't you run? What keeps you there?" The answer to these questions is what makes the actor able to function potently in the scene. Wanting to run away has the actor edging to-ward the door; he is virtually offstage for all the emotional commit-ment he gives a scene if that is his goal. And so often it is!

That is why instead of using *goal* or *motivation* or any of those customary acting terms, I use "What are you fighting *for*?" The actor must find a positive motivation, since it will serve him in a more forceful, stronger, more emotional way than a negative choice will. The character may appear negative or languid on the surface, but the actor can't settle for this appearance; he must dig deeper into what motivates the character in the strongest, most positive terms. The story of Chekhov's THE THREE SISTERS is not about three sisters who didn't make it to Moscow; it's about fighting like hell to get there all through the play.

In Chekhov—in many plays—a character will claim, "I am bored," but an actor cannot play boredom or he will be boring. He must find what it is the character wants instead of the boring condition he's in, and he must fight for that. I use the word *fight* because the actor must find the strongest, most positive goal possible. Nothing less will do.

An actor must make the most active choice possible for every scene. There is no passive scene, none that belongs to another character if you are in it, none where you support and someone else stars: these are old-fashioned show business concepts that don't help make a truthful and integrated production. Only by each actor making the strongest choice of what *he* is fighting for in every scene can a play come to life.

How, then, do you achieve balance if everyone is in there pitching hard for what he's fighting for? Through relationship. Through the give and take of relationship, through consideration for the other characters in the scene, through your sensitivity to their reaction to what you fight for, through an increased awareness of the others and how you affect them and how they affect you: a heightening of the awarenesses you have in life toward other people.

An actor is looking for conflict. Conflict is what creates drama. Plays are not written about our everyday lives or the moments of peace and placidity but about the extraordinary, the unusual, the climaxes. I am always surprised at how actors try to iron out the conflict that may lurk below the surface of a scene, flattening it instead of heightening it. Perhaps we are taught so thoroughly in our everyday lives to avoid trouble that actors don't realize they must go looking for it. The more conflict they find, the more interesting the performance of the play.

Maximum conflict is what you should be looking for. Who is interfering with your getting what you are fighting for? Do battle with her, fight her, woo her, charm her, revile her. Find as many *ways* as you can to go about getting what you are fighting for. The more ways you find, the more interesting your performance will be. Isn't variety still the spice of life?

All of life is a fight: we always *want* something. Even in our deepest despairs, when we feel like jumping off the top of the Empire State Building, we still want something and have been thwarted from getting it. We all know that there's a lot of thwarting in life, and plays are written about it. What seems like defeat is always just another way of fighting. The suicide fights the whole world for not having given him what he wants, the murderer just kills one. But we always want something, we are always fighting, no matter how guised the action may be. The actor needs to find out what the basic fight is in every character in every scene. The various *ways* in which that fight is waged are what heighten the interest.

Remember: All of the guideposts are ways of creating and carrying out relationship. What more vivid way to create relationship than to instill it with what you are fighting for!

EXAMPLE: *What you are fighting for in the relationship*

THE GLASS MENAGERIE *by* TENNESSEE WILLIAMS

Amanda comes home after having discovered that her crippled daughter, Laura, has for some weeks not been attending the secretarial school in which Amanda enrolled her and for which she paid the tuition. Laura has left the house each day, pretending to go to the school, but she cannot because the place embarrasses her, as does her crippled foot. So instead she spends her days in the park, in the library. I question the two actresses who have just read the scene.

MS   Laura, what is your relationship to Amanda?

LAURA   She's my mother. So of course I love her very much. I'd like to please her.

MS   Is she right about sending you to the secretarial school?

L   Yes. I was very bad not to go.

MS   Then you are entirely in the wrong?

L   Yes. I should learn how to earn a living. She's trying to help me.

MS   Is secretarial school the only way you could learn to earn a living.

L   Yes.

MS   If you are guilty and wrong about everything, what are you right about?

L   I love her and my brother.

MS   What do you want for yourself?

L   To please my mother.

MS   Good. What else?

L   That's all.

MS   What about pleasing yourself?

L   Pleasing my mother would please me.

MS   Fine. I accept that. But need something more, something for you.

L   But that's all I want.

MS   You're limiting the character. Have you no dreams?

L   Oh. I see. Yes, I dream that Jim, the Gentleman Caller, will come and ask me to marry him. That would please my mother and it would also please me.

MS   Then you wouldn't have to learn to type.

L   Right.

MS   So consider that perhaps your mother is wrong to force you to learn to type. You go to the library, the park, you look in the windows at flowers. You could work in a florist shop or a library, and you wouldn't have to type.

L   But people would see me. They would see that I limp.

MS   They see you now, when you go to the park, the library; there are people there who see you.

L   But they don't know who I am.

MS   Do you not want to be known?

L   No. I'm very shy.

MS   Ah, that's the problem! Your're very shy. How do you, as an actress, handle that?

L   I'm afraid to look at people, my eyes go down to the floor, I hold on to my hands, I talk very softly.

MS   Do you hear what you've said? A whole list of negative actions, none of which will help you in the reading one whit. In rehearsal they might be useful physical expressions of shyness to be carefully worked out with the director, but for a reading they're nothing but inhibitions. Nothing to work *for*—just a list of downs.

L   But Laura is very shy, she's terrified of her mother, other people do frighten her.

MS   All true. All of no use to you in doing an audition. Do you know what I saw? An actress looking down at the floor, standing pigeon-toed, whom I couldn't hear. An actress who seemed dull and half-dead, spiritless, with no humor, no charm, no appeal. Do you expect me to hire such an actress for my play?

L   Was it that bad?

MS   It was that bad. It's the way actresses usually read for Laura, which is what makes it such a hard role to cast. It's filled with traps, this role, and you fell in all of them.

L   What should I do?

MS   All of those negative qualities you listed can only be effective as *opposites* to a great need in you that you are *fighting for*. The Laura that you describe gave up a long time ago; she's dead. Do I want to see a play about a hopeless, deadened girl? Yet this is the Laura actresses love to present. Tell me what you could be fighting for?

L   Love.

MS   From whom?

L   From the Gentleman Caller.

MS   That's fine, but he doesn't happen to be in this scene. Your mother is.

L   But she does love me.

MS   In the right way?

L   Oh. She should love me the way I think she should love me?

MS   Right. It's hard getting you to come up with something positive, isn't it? Try a little harder.

L   Okay. I want her to listen to what I want, which is to be allowed to work in a florist shop or with children. I'd love to work with children! An office would frighten me, but I'd be lovely with children. Yes, that's what I should get my mother to realize: my place is with children.

MS   Excellent. Do you see now, Laura, that we don't live for the realities but for the fantasies, the dreams of what might be. If we lived for reality, we'd be dead, every last one of us. Only dreams keep us going.

L   So all through this scene I should be fighting to get Amanda to see *me* instead of her image of me, I should be fighting to tell her what would make me happy. So I'm not wrong about hating to go to that secretarial school, she is. I feel bad because I let her down and because I lied to her, but if she'd just listen to my dreams of what I want, I wouldn't have had to lie to her. She's a very strong, domineering woman, my mother, and I've got to learn to stand up to her or I'll never get to work with children, where I'd be useful, I'd be so happy.

I'll tell you another secret dream: I think if I got to work with children, some man would come along, some man who lost his wife, and he'd see how good I am with children and he'd fall in love with me and we'd get married.

MS   Beautiful. Now you know what you're fighting for in the scene. Now you know what the emotional relationship is with your mother.

Amanda, how do you feel about your daughter?

AMANDA   I love her dearly, she worries me to death, she's so impractical, she doesn't know how to take care of herself, she's such a dreamer. I'm the one who has to be realistic, even though I don't want to be, but both of my children are such idealistic dreamers with not one ounce of common sense between them.

MS   Very good. What are you fighting for?

A   For her to come to her senses and see that she's got to earn a living.

MS   And are you right about how?

A   Absolutely.

MS   That's all I saw in the scene. That you were right and everyone else was wrong. Particularly Laura. So I saw a strident woman screaming and hollering, filled with indignation, bursting with self-pity.

A   Those things are true about Amanda!

MS   Right. They are. If that had been only half of what I saw, fine. But it was *all*.

A   So what did I leave out?

MS   You left out your need for Laura.

A   I need her to get some common sense.

MS   More. That, yes, but more.

A   I need to try to understand her. What is going on inside that head? Ah, mystery and secret, yes? She's very mysterious and hidden to me, always hiding, so I'd like to find out what goes with her. Yes, that's good.

MS   Very good. What was missing was a feeling that you loved her, that you were curious about her. All I saw was a know-it-all lady but no wonderment.

A   I understand. I thought of another thing I need from Laura: a sense of romance. I have these dreams of Laura finding a husband, some marvelous man who will take care of her. I was a very romantic girl, very pretty with lots of beaux, and it hurts me deeply to see that Laura has no suitors, but if she could just find one man, one sensitive enough to overlook her limp and to realize her lovely fine qualities, then I could rest content.

MS   That's wonderful. Why didn't you put it in the scene?

A   I was trying to be strong. I though all that stuff would be mushy and weak.

MS   That's why there's so little romance in our world now: everyone thinks romance is weak. Yet romance is everyone's secret dream—it's why we're alive. Never distrust romance; nothing could be stronger. If you had put that into the scene, Amanda would be dimensional, full and rich and appealing. Always look for the opposites. Trust that romance is strong. Tenderness is stronger than screaming. Whenever you have two considerations, which seem to cancel each other out, *do both*.

EXAMPLE: *Find many ways to fight for what you want*

A PALM TREE IN A ROSE GARDEN *by* MEADE ROBERTS

Barbara and Charlie have one of those "arrangement" relationships, which means that it is convenient for Charlie but Barbara isn't sure what future it has. For the present she has someone to be close to and she gets to go to Hollywood parties. This scene takes place after one of those parties, when she discovers Charlie has plans and ambitions that don't include her: he's going off to Rome with a producer, and he hasn't asked the producer to give Barbara a part in the film. The actors did a very impressive reading of the scene; it was dramatic and explosive. She created a relationship of need, but he, while very strong and dominant, had no warmth, nor was he very likable. We talk, trying always to find ways to deepen and enrich the work.

MS   What are your relationship choices?

BARBARA   I need him. I need him desperately, for my career, because I think he can help me there. I need him because I am lonely and he bolsters me up and gives me courage to go on fighting to be an actress.

MS   Are you in love with him?

B   We're supposed to have a sensible, friendship arrangement. I do get to rely on him too much; he becomes the center of my existence.

MS   Very good choice; that's why the scene worked so well. But you're not in love with him?

B   I love him but I'm not *in* love with him.

MS   Why not?

B I know he prefers men.

MS What's that got to do with it?

B It would be useless to fall in love with him.

MS Women fall in love with homosexuals all the time.

B I'm not that kind of woman. I know too much about men like that.

MS Do you see what you're doing when you say that? You're limiting yourself when you say "I'm not the kind of person who would do that." You rule out a strong emotional choice you could have made in the scene.

B You mean it would even be stronger if a woman like me, who knows homosexuals well from the work I'm in, nonetheless falls in love with one? It's going to surprise me even more because I thought I was immune to that trap—and here I find myself in it. Yes, I see that would be a very useful choice. Besides, there's something in women that makes them think they can reform a homosexual and show him the true way, isn't there?

MS In some women it seems very strong.

B Why I missed it is because in the scene I seem to take his sexual preferences so much for granted. But that could just be my clever way of dealing with it, to get him on my side.

MS How did you conceive of using the drunkenness in the scene?

B It makes me blatant. I lose all pride, I beg for what I want.

MS Excellent. But I thought you used it as a down too much.

B How can you be up when you're drunk and your man is dumping you?

MS By playing a game: by insisting you've got a wonderful solution that will make him happy and make you happy. By playing the opposite to the lines that make you wallow and snivel and beg and plead. You did those things beautifully, but I missed the "up" that would have made your choices even better. Your work could have had a much greater range if you'd found the up, if you had found more ways to get him to do what you need. What you did was powerful, but it was predictable, after a while, because you failed to find enough humor in the scene, you didn't find enough games as ways to woo him, coax him, into taking you to Rome. Pretty soon it became a repeat of itself, and you can't afford that in a reading:

B you have to find as many ways of reaching him as you
can. You settled for too few.

B I could have used mystery and secret, too.

MS Yes indeed. How?

B I could have implied I know something that I'm not going to tell, that I won't tell anyone else if he'll just be nice
to me. I could do it in such a way as to frighten him but
all the while pretending that I'm always on his side and
that I would never do anything to hurt him. Of course I
would hurt him; I'd want to, to get even for the way he's
hurting me. I could have played these opposites in the
scene: I'll never hurt you—I sure will hurt you unless
you're nice to me. Then he'd never know what I was going to do next, and neither would the audience.

MS One of the great results of using opposites is behavior
that is unpredictable, therefore always more intriguing to
an audience. It's why people are forever astonishing us
in life: we don't know what they're going to do next, they
are not consistent, we're always being surprised by their
doing something we didn't expect. Interesting acting always has this risk element of the unpredictable in it.
That's why actors like Laurence Olivier and Marlon
Brando and De Niro and Pacino interest us so: we never
quite know what they're going to do next. They make us
want to know. They make us keep watching them. They
surprise us with their unpredictability.

The following was a discussion with the first actor who read the
role of Charlie:

MS What is your relationship to Barbara?

CHARLIE I She's an acquaintance.

MS Do you like her?

C I She drinks too much. She talks too much. Not much to
like there.

MS Then, why are you with her?

C I I wouldn't be with her, if it were me.

MS But you are with her, Charlie.

C I Girls who drink and get hysterical, that's not the kind of
girl I could ever like.

MS Then, why are you with her?

C I The script says so.

MS That reason is not going to be of much help to you, Charlie. Your job is to justify the situations of the script, to

motivate the actions of the character. Start with what you are fighting for in this relationship with Barbara.

C I He wants to get her off his back.

MS Who does?

C I Charlie does.

MS I thought you were Charlie.

C I No, I'm Joe. Charlie is the character.

MS My suggestion is that you call yourself "I" rather than talk about "he" when you approach a reading. Make it about yourself.

C I But I'm used to doing characters.

MS I know you are. I suggest you discard that habit and take up a new habit, which is to call yourself "I" instead of "he" when you do readings.

C I But it's not me in this scene. I'm nothing like this guy Charlie.

MS Exactly why you'll save a lot of time if you'll start out with insisting it *is* about you rather than about someone else. When you say "he," it already distances you from the character. With your insistence that you and Charlie are nothing alike, you are likely to fall into the trap of showing only the *differences* between you and him. That won't create Charlie, will it?

C I But we are as different as night and day.

MS That isn't going to help you get cast for the role, is it? That makes you a stranger to the role you are trying to create. Train yourself in the audition situation to think that every scene is about you, not about someone else. That's the quickest way to find motivations that will justify the actions in the scene.

C I If I can't do the character, then I'm just doing me every time.

MS Isn't that you on that stage every time you're up there?

C I Yes, of course it is me, but it's me as somebody else.

MS That "somebody else" is what you work to find during the rehearsal period of a play, but you can't do that in a reading. Be practical: how can you "do the character" if you have only ten minutes to look at the scene?

C I With some characters, I identify right away; so that system would work then. But with others that are so far from me, I have to work out something. Like this Charlie, he's a fruit, he loves other guys. I'm not like that. How can I use myself?

MS   You're an actor, yet you cannot *imagine* yourself loving a man?

C I   Never in a million years.

MS   All right; perhaps that is not essential to this scene. Can't you instead concern yourself with the conflict between your love and friendship for Barbara and your wanting to be close to a producer who will give you a role in a film that does not include her?

C I   I could never like a girl like Barbara and I could never sleep with anyone to get a role.

MS   You're going to have big trouble being an actor, with all the limitations you set for yourself. Can't you expand your concepts about yourself?

C I   I can't identify with this character in any way! I'd hate to be like this Charlie. I would never put up with that girl treating me like that. Never!

MS   That explains why we saw nothing but disdain in your attitude toward her—no sympathy, no love for her, no consideration of her feelings. All we saw was a tough guy treating a girl like shit. It was very strong, what you did, but it was all on one note: it had no dimension, no closeness, no tenderness, no sensitivity to what her feelings might be. That is the danger in readings if you refuse to put yourself into the situation: you strike an attitude, you become one-note Johnny, you have no dimension—and you don't get hired. By your refusal to use yourself, because you operated out of a judgment of the character instead of an identification and a justification of Charlie, you had no opposites at all in what you did.

C I   You said to use me. I used me. I'm not at all like Charlie.

MS   You must use you *plus* the situation of the play. To put yourself in this situation means giving yourself Charlie's reactions to Barbara and finding ways to justify them, to motivate them. But if you make a judgment of Charlie that is so unsympathetic, then of course you are blinded to the possibilities of justifying.

C I   But I think he's wrong in everything he does.

MS   You wouldn't think that if *you* were in that situation: if Barbara were a very dear friend, whom you liked a lot, maybe more than anyone else, if she'd been good to you and helped you a lot and you owed her consideration. Then you'd put up with the way she acts in this scene, you would feel sorry for her, you would try to help her.

C I I wouldn't help anybody, not if she acted like that to me.

MS Not even if you cared about the person more than anyone else in the world?

C I Well, maybe.

MS That's why I always suggest you use love as the feeling
you have for the other character. Then you can justify
the actions of the character. Then you can find opposites.

      Instead, all you did, out of your judgment of the
character, was to use your tough, disapproving side. You
found in the scene no reason to use your sensitive, romantic side. That's a part of you, too. You failed to use
your imagination; you used only literalism. You refused
to budge from your disapproval. You did not use your
fantasy life, only your everyday image of yourself.

      I doubt that Brando or Pacino or any of the actors
you yourself have said you admire would have trouble
identifying with Charlie's kind of sexual or emotional
life. As a matter of fact, in DOG DAY AFTERNOON, Pacino
did do a Charlie, didn't he?

      Perhaps you shouldn't be an actor at all, if it is true
that you cannot put yourself into the emotional life of a
person who's unlike you.

      Let's try another actor and see what choices he
would make in the scene.

The new Charlie and I had this talk:

MS What did you decide your relationship is to Barbara?

CHARLIE II She's very valuable to me because she cares about me
and she's someone I can take places instead of going
alone. A man like me in a place like Hollywood needs
someone to date whom he can trust and rely on, who
won't make a fuss every time she sees you looking at
a man or some man looking at you. I think she's been
very tactful and understanding, up until tonight.

MS What causes the trouble tonight?

C II I have to make a choice between her and someone else.
I don't want to hurt her, but it's her life or mine.

MS Why can't you take her with you?

C II This producer is interested in me, and he's not interested in her. I can't jeopardize his interest in me by ask-

ing him to take her to Rome, too. That would really queer things. If you'll pardon the phrase.

MS   Do you think she's justified in her feelings?

C II   Sure. I was using her and now I'm dumping her.

MS   Aren't you rather hard on yourself?

C II   I think it's true, and that's why I feel so bad. I feel guilty about mistreating her. Of course there's also an opposite: I never promised her a rose garden, did I? I'd like to help her out, but I can't do it if it means injury to me. You've got to take care of number one. Besides, she gets drunk and unpleasant and that upsets me.

MS   You were using her, you said. Was she using you?

C II   Oh, sure. She got what she wanted. Or almost. Trouble is, she began wanting me, and I couldn't give her that. Everything else, but not that. So in that way what she wanted from me was unfair, it was more than I ever said I could give her. So there's a lot of conflict in the scene for me: not wanting to hurt her but wanting to protect my own interests at the same time.

MS   What are the ways in which you fight for what you need?

C II   I try to keep it from her at first. I try to kid her along, like it was just another date and I'll see her tomorrow. But then she knows something's up, so I try to evade her probing me. Then I have to admit it. So I try to let her down gently, then I have to get firm. I play innocent, then I admit I'm guilty; I play little boy, I play stern father, I play injured friend, I play misunderstood lover.

MS   The way you shifted from one role to another as she revealed her new tactics to get at you was very effective. We never knew for sure what you might do next. I think that makes acting most interesting.

C II   I also feel I have to be very careful with her, because she could do something dangerous if I hurt her badly enough.

MS   What could she do to hurt you?

C II   She could go make a scene with the producer. But she gets me so mad because she's so demanding, so unreasonable. I wanted to slug her at one point. Then I had to control myself and act like a pussycat with her. I came close to slugging her.

MS   It's the playing off of one impulse against the other that made your work in the scene so good. What I didn't see enough of was humor.

C II   I panic when I do readings. I think, I can't take up too much time—the auditors are impatient, I've got to get on with it—so I rush through like an express train, and that makes me leave out humor.

MS   Why?

C II   Humor is a relaxation to me. It means you stop for a minute to see how ridiculous you are or she is, how absurd this situation we've got ourselves into. I'm afraid to stop for that.

MS   What are you afraid of?

C II   That the auditors will say "Thank you very much."

MS   But you aren't going to stop literally, are you, to find humor? It will be a part of what you're doing.

C II   I know you're right, but I think of it as stopping because I have to think about putting it in, and I think thinking is stopping.

MS   We all think while we're talking.

C II   I wish I could convince myself of that. But I get into a panic at readings.

MS   That is why your reading was sometimes like buckshot being fired all over the place with no focus. And you would sometimes lose awareness of Barbara and start shouting and carrying on all by yourself.

C II   I know. I know. I know. If I could just get over that panic . . . I think my readings would be a lot better.

MS   What causes you to panic, you say, is fear of taking time and making the auditors impatient. Think of it this way: The auditors are going to be impatient anyhow, so what's the difference? They will be far less impatient if you make your points clearly, if you keep focused on your target (which is your partner), and if you use yourself more.

C II   I thought I was using myself.

MS   A lot. Not entirely. I note that in life you have a lot of humor. You scarcely do anything without humor. Yet you get up on the stage to read and leave it behind. That means you're not using *all* of yourself, doesn't it? In your life if you got yourself into a pickle like this one with a Barbara, there'd be a lot of humor!

C II   I would like, if I may, to say something about the problem the other Charlie was having.

MS   Sure.

C II   I didn't have the problem he had in the scene because I should think loving a man is no different from loving a woman, so I would just use the same feelings I had for a woman. Besides, to me the scene wasn't about my loving a man, it was about how I should deal with my friend Barbara, whom I like a lot. But I have blocks in other scenes just as severe as he did for this scene.

MS   A block usually comes from a prejudice.

C II   We all have prejudices.

MS   Sure. We have to admit we've got them and find a way to deal with them. But refusing to use your imagination isn't dealing with the problem. It's being defeatist; it's limiting you in ways you don't need to be limited.

C II   Does that mean we can all play all roles?

MS   Absolutely not. If I were an actor, I could never in a million years play Stanley Kowalski in STREETCAR NAMED DESIRE. Probably neither could you. But that doesn't mean we couldn't imagine how Stanley feels. We could never be Stanley physically—and, of course, that's frequently an essential element in casting—but we could understand his wanting to be king of his own home, his resenting Blanche for upsetting Stella and acting superior, we could understand his attraction to Blanche coupled with his despising her fine airs. I think if we really try to use our own feelings to the fullest extent of our imagination, drawing on our fantasy lives instead of limiting ourselves to our literal reality lives, we can find feelings in *anyone* we can recognize and make real. We can do little to change how we look and what that has done to mold our personalities, but if we deal with inner feelings instead of outer silhouette, we can give an intelligent, satisfying reading.

   If we make every reading a true projection of an act of creative imagination, it is possible auditors will begin to change physical requirements in order to hire us. They've sure done that for Laurence Olivier, haven't they?

EXAMPLE

A LITTLE NIGHT MUSIC *by* **HUGH WHEELER,** based on the Ingmar Bergman screenplay for SMILES OF A SUMMER NIGHT

The opening scene between the young man and his new stepmother, who's his age. I ask the actors some questions:

MS   What is your relationship?

YOUNG MAN   She's my stepmother.

MS   That's a fact. Facts don't help much. What is the emotional relationship?

YM   I'm attracted to her.

MS   How much?

YM   Oh, I find her pretty.

MS   How much: Pretty isn't enough, is it?

YM   She drives me crazy. I can hardly stand it, being near
her. I want to grab her and kiss her and hold her in
my arms.

MS   Fine! Now we're getting somewhere.

YM   But this is the first scene between them. If I make
that choice now, I won't have anywhere to go.

MS   Nonsense. Actors are always holding back because
they "won't have anywhere to go." You have to start
out mad for her in the moment before or it becomes
a scene about your having to practice on your viola
and she needs to get some knitting done. You need
to create the fantasy of what you want, and that is
what will drive you through the scene. If the fantasy
of desiring her is strong enough and you create the
opposite that you adore your father, so it's forbidden
because you would never want to hurt him, then you
have a line strong enough to drive you through the
entire play.

YM   I thought in the first scene I would make the *discovery* that I am attracted to her.

MS   That is the difference between doing the play and
doing an audition. You have nothing to use in your
moment before then: you're just a young man who
comes on the scene to practice his music and gets interrupted by his stepmother. It's not enough of an
emotional investment for you to carry you through a
reading. Of course, you can still use that discovery,
but make it more urgent: I discover that I am so attracted to her that I can hardly remember my music,
I'm in real trouble, I think I can't resist her. That is
a discovery of importance for the scene.

YM   What if they ask me to read the second scene? What

will I use then if I've used up my attraction for her in the first scene?

MS Attractions to someone don't get "used up"—not if they are love, not if they are needful, not if they are emotional rather than just sexual. Attractions that are emotional *grow*; you get more attracted to her in each scene; it becomes more and more difficult to restrain yourself; your consideration for your father becomes more secondary to your need to embrace your stepmother. The conflict deepens, becomes traumatic—you're ready to kill yourself if you can't have her. You see, you always have the conflict of your father to use as an opposite, a repression on the emotion in the scene, so you can afford to go all out with desiring her and then the next moment use censoring yourself: No, I mustn't do that. Think of it in the extremes of kissing her in a mad embrace and then dropping her as if she were fire burning you because of your guilt. If these extreme emotions are *underneath* the scene, then the games you play with her will have meaning because the stakes mean something to you.

STEPMOTHER But surely I'm not in love with him in this first scene. I'm just newly a bride! And he's my stepson.

MS Which gives you more to act with, being in love with him or just finding him rather cute and pleasant?

S Being in love with him. But it doesn't seem right to me.

MS Later on in the play you do discover you are so madly in love with him that you run away together, so you desert your husband, right?

S But I'm not at that point yet.

MS But in order to get to that point, you have to be in love with him now. The character may not know it, but the love must exist in her subconscious; the actress has always to know more than the character. This is a good example of why: if you don't *know* that you're in love with the boy, then you haven't got going for you in the scene what is subconsciously driving the character to flirt with him in the first place.

S So I use that I am in love with him, but I am shocked by it and try to control it. That is a stronger choice, isn't it? So I play these little teasing games with him to find out how he feels about me.

MS   Excellent choice. Then your games have a purpose. And if ever it gets too far out of hand, you always have the opposite to use of "I shouldn't do this" or "I mustn't let my feelings rule."

For audition purposes, you've got to go for the maximum involvement in the relationship. Ask the question "Am I in love with him?" and don't ever hesitate to make the answer be *yes*. To say no to that question gives you only a superficial attraction to work with; to say yes gives you a true emotional life commitment to work with. Clearly that is the valuable one for an actor.

EXAMPLE

ORPHEUS DESCENDING *by* TENNESSEE WILLIAMS

Val is an itinerant stud who's trying to find a way out of playing around like an adolescent and into being an adult. Lady is an older woman, whose husband is dying upstairs; she runs the store, she is lonely, and she offers Val a job. I ask the actor what he was fighting for:

VAL   Well, I need a place to sleep and I need to get some bread.

MS   Then there's nothing personal in your approach to Lady? Anyone who gave you bread and a bed would do.

V   Sure.

MS   Is that the most valuable choice you can make?

V   She's an old broad. What would I want with her?

MS   You say in the scene you're giving up playing around with kids. Doesn't that mean you might be attracted now, for the first time, to an older woman? Who owns something, who has something more to offer you than a one-night stand? Who interests you in a new way, in a way different from other attractions you've had in your life, who represents the possibility of commitment, who might answer needs that are more than merely sexual?

V   I didn't think of that.

MS   Which gives you more to work with?

V   Being attracted to her, being curious about her, seeing how
we might work out something together.

MS That's what I mean by looking for the *most* you can find in
a relationship. You picked the minimum. If you find you're
choosing mere practicality, it's not going to be enough:
You've got to add the dream of wanting something more from
life, and this person is the one who might give it to you.

Then I ask the actress what her relationship is to Val:

LADY   He's a big stud type and I think he's sexy, but he also means
trouble to me.

MS With those interesting opposites, what is the relationship?

L   He turns me on. Maybe I'd like to go to bed with him.

MS Do you want any more than bed?

L   What more could you expect from a roving stud like him?

MS You tell me.

L   I'd be a fool to expect anything more.

MS Then be a fool. Dream. Dreams are always foolish.

L   You mean I'd think of settling down with him? He's so much
younger than I am, he's irresponsible, he just bums around,
he doesn't know how to run a store, what could he give me?

MS Love. Respect. Partnership. He could attract all the women
in the vicinity to come to the store to buy things, but if he
just wanted you, think how you'd be the envy of everyone in
town. If he was tired of bumming around and ready to settle
down, you could offer him what he's never had: warmth, a
chance to earn a respectable living, a commitment from you,
tenderness and concern, motherliness, a roof over his head
that's paid for, a chance to live a decent life at last.

L   If I offered him that, I could expect a commitment from a man
like this?

MS If you give him all that, you just might get something very
good back. You should take the risk. That is what we hope
for, isn't it?

The moral: Don't settle for anything less than the biggest dream
for your future. That's what you should want from a relationship. Put
all that longing into the moment before, and ignite it with the spark
of two people sensually meeting for the first time. Fight to make the
dream come true.

Guidepost 3: The Moment Before

Every scene you will ever act begins in the middle, and it is up to you, the actor, to provide what comes before.

This is true if you do a scene at the beginning of a play or the middle of a play or the end of the play. Something always precedes what you are doing. I call this something *the moment before*.

In the audition situation most actors come onstage to read for a role with very little moment before. The result is that it takes them most of the reading to get warmed up. By the time they are, they've lost the attention of the auditors. Never does an actor need the moment before more desperately than in the audition situation.

But an actor needs a fully developed moment before every time he steps onstage to start a scene. You've seen many of these performances where we say, "He wasn't so good at first, but after he got going he was fine." A good actor doesn't wait to get going; he comes on with it because he already had it going in the wings.

In order to create this moment before, before he enters, the actor may have to go back ten or twenty years in the life of the character. You can't do George or Martha in WHO'S AFRAID OF VIRGINIA WOOLF without considering the length of their marriage, how it started, and what point it's at now, but you also can't get going in any scene in that devilish play without a strong, well-defined *moment* that applies to the scene you are about to do and no other. There are many generalizations one can make about a character and his life, just as there are about George or Martha: George's feeling of failure, fanned by Martha's need to be on top; the ever-gnawing presence of Martha's daddy and the university in which they exist; Martha's need to make it with other men in order to prove she does not need George and George alone. All of this information, if it leads to emotion, will help, but it must all lead to *specific* choices about how these generalizations affect the moment before your scene begins. What does the marriage, Daddy, the university, teaching, sex, love, have to do with what you feel at this very moment about George, about Nick and his slender bride, about yourself? What are you fighting for in the relationship in the scene you are about to read, and exactly where are your feelings at this specific moment before?

I find actors tend to work with generalizations. They fail to apply all the analysis they are fond of doing, the information they have gathered, to the specific moments of the scene. The more *specific*, the more focused the moment before, the better the entire scene will go.

The moment before requires an important emotional commitment from the actor. Not his mind, for that is never enough; in acting the mind is only useful if it guides a person to his feelings. It's not enough to think about what the moment before should be; one has to seep oneself in it, drown in it, be overcome by it.

I liken the actor's job in creating the moment before to priming a motor to get it started. You have to do a number on yourself, you have to talk to yourself, flay yourself into feeling, so that you are aching to get on that stage and start to fight. You want to be propelled on by your feelings, not led daintily by your head. (Yes, this applies to THE IMPORTANCE OF BEING EARNEST or DESIGN FOR LIVING, too. Underneath every human being's rational cool exterior is passion. You won't find the reason a human being creates a style for himself unless you find the passion in him that drives him to need such a cover.)

When an actor goes for an audition to do a reading for the auditors (who may be the director, the producer, the playwright, the musical director, the choreographer, the casting director, associate directors and producers—any or all of these people), the first impression he makes is the strongest one, so he had better make a good first impression. When an actor comes onstage in a performance, the first impression he makes is a lasting one on the audience. It had better be an impressive impression.

It is very much like shaking hands with someone when we are introduced for the first time. That limp paw laid in your hand like a wet fish creates a first impression that may take that person months to change.

The actor wants his first impression to be the right one. That requires the right moment before and his full emotional commitment to this moment. Only with this firm basis can he begin to develop the scene and in turn develop a whole performance in a play. The moment before must be strong, meaty, and full; it's got to give the actor something to feed on all through the scene. There is no rehearsal to give the actor security, so he must use his own life, his own inner life, his own fantasy life, his own imaginative life, which he invests in a moment before that is greatly meaningful to him. When this moment before is richly invested, it can be the substitute for the rehearsal. It can carry the actor through the reading of material he doesn't know well.

EXAMPLE

THE HEIRESS *by* RUTH AND AUGUSTUS GOETZ, based on the Henry James novel *Washington Square*

In the scene between Catherine and her aunt, Catherine hopes to elope that night with the fortune hunter, Morris Townsend. The scene opens with Catherine alone on stage, packed and waiting for Morris to arrive. Every sound she hears coming from the street she thinks is the arrival of Morris. She is excited and brimming over with expectation: tonight her entire life will change, she will leave her oppressive, domineering father forever and start a wonderful new life with the man she loves. The actress must come onstage with all of these fantasy expectations rich and full, or the beginning of the scene is flat and mundane. Further, it is the creation of these beautiful fantasies of the future, opposed to the reality of living with a father who considers her a dull and colorless dolt of a girl, that must underlie the entire scene. Without the creation of these in the moment before, it is impossible to create the various events and discoveries of the scene:

That her aunt, being so excited by the romantic prospect, wants to come along on the elopement;

That she will at last get revenge on her despised father;

That her aunt shares the father's view that Catherine is a dull girl;

That her aunt thinks Catherine has ruined her chances of marriage by revealing to Morris that she will be disinherited if she elopes;

That the money left to her by her mother will not be sufficient to support her intended husband in the style to which he has aspired;

That Morris is indeed not going to come that night, or ever;

That she is left forever in this house on Washington Square, to endure living with a father who considers her dreary and whom she loathes;

That her aunt pities her.

But not one of this series of discoveries and events can occur fully unless the moment before has the excitement of expectation that a lifetime's dream is going to come true *now*. In the moment before, the actress must create this dream, must feel the urgency of it happening now for her. You can't wander onstage to do this scene without a strong, full romantic moment before.

For the aunt, there must be an equally strong moment before:

What is that noise? What is Catherine up to?—boundless curiosity, a desire to be a part of her romance, a need to keep Catherine from harming herself. The strongest element that must dominate the moment before for the aunt is her wanting romance for Catherine, because then the aunt's lifetime investment in this plain girl will pay off and justify her faith. It is important to make the aunt's involvement with Catherine one of deep love and a need to live vicariously through the girl, since her own life is so empty now that her husband is dead, now that she has lost her own home and her own place in the world, now that she is reduced to living as the poor relation with the snobbish and superior Dr. Sloper.

EXAMPLE

SUDDENLY LAST SUMMER *by* TENNESSEE WILLIAMS

The girl is entering her aunt's garden, where she is to meet and be interrogated by the doctor who will determine her future life—or death in life, because unless she can convince him that her story of cannibalism is true, he will perform a lobotomy on her. The past rushes in on her, the sound of the Waring blender meaning Aunt Violet's five o'clock daiquiri is being prepared, as always; she confronts the vision of her future, forever gardenless and in shadows if the doctor fails to believe her incredible tale. All around her in this beautiful garden is the evidence of wealth and power and ease, against which she must fight for her life. The determination to fight must be very strongly created in the moment before, so that the garden can take full frightening effect. The stronger the fight, the stronger the garden as her archenemy. The actress who creates these opposite forces in the moment before has a chance to create a very strong reading, filled with drama and conflict—and the desire to communicate.

EXAMPLE

THE MIDDLE OF THE NIGHT *by* PADDY CHEYEVSKY

The young wife is longing to see her husband, desperate for the resurgence of her desire for him, to re-create the memory of those wonderful sexual experiences she has not had in so long. Most actresses merely create irritation, since the opening lines are: "What are you doing here? I told you I didn't want to see you. I want a divorce." Since these rejections of him are so strongly written, it is the opposite—her positive pull toward him—that the actress needs to create in the moment before. She must feel the conflict of finding herself still desiring her sexual young stud of a husband while she has pledged herself to a caring relationship with a much older man. If this desire for the husband is not created, there is no dramatic conflict in the scene, just an obdurate actress standing there saying "Go away" over and over and over again. Why does the scene exist? It can only be tiresome and reiterative unless the wife is strongly attracted to the husband. If that is not created in the moment before, it is never likely to crop up in the scene at all. Result: no scene.

EXAMPLE

THE SUBJECT WAS ROSES *by* FRANK GILROY

That splendid scene between the boy and his stepmother, in which they fight over the rightful interpretation of the father's place in both their lives, will never reach the moving crescendo it deserves unless the moment before is richly filled by both actors. The day the mother has dreamed of for years has finally come true: her son is home from the army and she can live again. But what is this dreadful numbing fear that gnaws at her subconscious, fear that her son has changed, that he may not want her anymore, that he is siding with his father instead of with her, that he will not fulfill her dreams. The sleepless night in which the son turns over and over his realization that he has misjudged his father through his entire life; that his mother and he created an impregnable wall against the father, shutting him out; that he must convince his mother of their wrongdoing so they can both make amends and change their estimate and their entire treatment of the man.

The Mother: "I must fight to keep my son against his father, who will try to steal him away from me."

The Son: "I must fight to get my mother to revalue my father. We must change our ways and make it up to him."

It is difficult to do any reading without creating a moment before that takes into account what you are fighting for in the relationship. When an actor becomes adept at using the guideposts in the reading situation, he can combine the first three (as in the preceding sentence) to achieve a strong incentive to throw himself into the scene he is to read.

Guidepost 4: Humor

Humor is not jokes. It is that attitude toward being alive without which you would long ago have jumped off the Fifty-ninth Street Bridge.

Humor is not being funny. It is the coin of exchange between human beings that makes it possible for us to get through the day. Humor exists even in the humorless.

There is humor in every scene, just as there is in every situation in life. There is humor in Chekhov (too seldom found) and even in Eugene O'Neill (virtually never found). When we say about a life situation, "And it's not funny, either," we are attempting to inject humor into a situation that lacks it. We *try* in life to put humor everywhere; if we didn't, we couldn't bear to live.

One would sometimes think actors are trying to reverse the life process by what they do onstage. They take humor out instead of put it in. That's what makes acting unlifelike. I have trouble believing in the seriousness of a scene in which there is no humor; it is unlike life. And yet actors will say to me, "How can I find humor in this scene? It's very serious!" For the exact same reason one would be driven to find humor in the same situation in life: because it is deadly serious and human beings cannot bear all that heavy weight, they alleviate the burden by humor.

Sometimes we lighten the burden for others because of the weight we are dumping on them, which we know is more than they can possibly want. Sometimes we lighten the burden for ourselves. Either way, the heavier the situation, the more we are needful of humor to endure it.

Even Neil Simon has humor, among all those jokes.

I find it fascinating that so many actors have trouble putting humor into their acting. Of course, many actors do it instinctively, and in all fine acting it is a major ingredient. But where the instincts are being interfered with, the actor must become *conscious* of humor and look for it; if it's not there, then he must learn to put it there. Humorless acting is the dreariest kind: it's the hallmark of soap opera performing—and even there humor is likely to creep in, however half-heartedly and apologetically. "Sorry to smile at this, old boy, because I am taking this in deadly earnestness, but I did want to let you know I'm human."

It's difficult to *learn* humor. It's one of those you've-got-it-or-you-don't qualities. But since I contend every life situation has humor and every scene in every play has humor, it must follow that all human beings have humor, however dispirited or mean or tiny or unconscious. Fan that tiny flame; it could grow into something. I note actors not using humor onstage who are perfectly capable of expressing some of it in their lives; they simply don't know what it is because they've never thought about it. Humor, they are sure, occurs in comedies. If they aren't acting in a comedy, they don't have to concern themselves with humor. I venture to say humor is more important in a drama than a comedy. At least in a comedy all the actors are looking for it, albeit all too often over-zealously. One of the reasons comedies are so often unamusing is because the actors are working hard for jokes instead of finding the real-life humor.

Examples of humor are best culled from performances by actors you admire.

In the honey-tongued THE LION IN WINTER, would the remarkable performances of Katharine Hepburn and Peter O'Toole have seemed half so memorable without the highly personalized and competitive humor they brought to those roles? Think, seriously think, of seeing Eleanor and Henry up on that giant screen played totally without humor.

Or Hepburn and Bogart in THE AFRICAN QUEEN. Without their idiosyncratic humor, would that film be indelible on our memories?

Take Hepburn and Bogart in any of their films. Are they not "living legends," still providing endless fascination to newcomers and to all ages because of their humor? Not their humor alone, of course, but their humor allied to their particular passions, their kind of dreaming, their invincible fight.

Cary Grant. Audrey Hepburn. Carole Lombard. Clark Gable. Claudette Colbert. Is it not their humor that made them so likable?

In today's performing, even glamorous figures like Robert Redford and Paul Newman and Barbra Streisand would not be able to command the world without the humor that makes them so attractive, seductive, irreplacable.

In DOG DAY AFTERNOON, would that outrageous and normally disapproved-of character have been so popular to the world were it not for Al Pacino's crazy, unpredictable humor?

Would Garbo be the romantic figure of all time without that mocking, self-deprecating quality that made her so mysterious, so attractive, so different from anyone else?

Would Dietrich's glamor be enough to carry her through an entire lifetime career without her sense of the absurdity of what she is doing? Her faint, sly caricature of herself—and of us for believing in her.

Would Laurence Olivier's RICHARD III be half so beguiling without that incredible humor that attracts us to the man we despise ourselves for being so attracted?

If Laurence Olivier is the greatest actor in our current world, it would not be so without his unique humor, which imbues every role with a flavor that only he can bring.

I've never seen a great or a star actor who did not have humor.

Guidepost 5: Opposites

Whatever you decide is your motivation in the scene, the opposite of that is also true and should be in it.

Through the years of teaching I have found that this concept of opposites is the most remarkable for actors. Once it permeates their thinking, they regard it as such an essential that they wonder how they existed before without it. In truth, they probably did not exist without it, but their consciousness level was very low and their ability to summon it when needed was minimal. But opposites exist so strongly in every human being that one would have difficulty avoiding it. Actors do try, however.

Consistency is the heart of dull acting. What fascinates us about other human beings, and particularly about splendid actors, is their inconsistency, their use of opposites. Yet for all its vital importance, I find opposites one of the most difficult guideposts to explain to actors. In the course of doing scenes, almost every actor comes to understand what opposites are and how to use them, but in theory it is frequently a murky concept to communicate. So though you may find opposites unclear in this explanation, you will find them eminently clear in the *doing*.

Think about a human being: in all of us there exists love and there exists hate, there exist creativity and an equal tendency toward self-destructiveness, there exist sleeping and waking, there exists night and there exists day, sunny moods and foul moods, a desire to love and a desire to kill. Since these extremities do exist in all of us, then they must also exist in each character in each scene. Not all opposites, of course, not this exhaustive listing I've just given, but some of them. If it is a love scene, there is bound to be hate in it too; if there is need, great need, for someone, we are bound to resent having that need. Both emotions should be in the scene; it is lopsided and untrue if only one is.

It is the actor's creation of opposites that develops conflict, and therefore drama, and therefore interest. For some unfathomable reason, actors are fond of bringing onstage the resolution of a conflict, which is tidy and dead, rather than the conflict itself, which is exciting. I suppose it is because in life we are trained to avoid conflict, run from confrontations, make our painful lives as easy as we can for ourselves. But it is the *process* of dealing with pain the actor must put on the stage, not the fact of having solved it.

The more *extreme* the opposites the actor chooses for a scene, the more everything in between is likely to occur instinctively, naturally, without the actor having to consider these choices. The choice of extreme opposites may often have to be made consciously in order to guarantee the wide range of emotion the actor can deal with in between. Watch a parent with his child: one moment he smothers the child in affection, the next moment he wants to beat her up because she is so vexing. It is that sort of range the actor should seek for every scene: I love you versus I could kill you. One of the reasons A TASTE OF HONEY is such an effective play is because it deals so successfully in the opposites of its characters. Helen, the mother, dances and sings joyfully one moment and breaks down in self-pity over her dreadful head cold the next; Jo, sullen and resentful of the new apartment one moment, kneels to create beauty with her flower bulbs the next. And so it goes all through this fascinating play. It is an object lesson in the use of opposites.

There are opposites in every scene. The actor may have to dig for them, for the playwright may well have implied them under the surface of the character and not have written them into the dialogue at all; but they are always there for the digging. They are well worth digging for; they result in the most interesting kind of acting: the complex.

EXAMPLE: *Why an actor needs to know himself in order to find opposites to his own strong feelings*

THE SUBJECT WAS ROSES *by* FRANK GILROY

A character actress and a young man read the big confrontation scene between the mother and son. The son has been away in the army; this scene takes place the morning after his return home. After saying good-bye to his father, he turns to have breakfast with his mother now realizing for the first time that he and his mother may have been unfair in their judgments of his father, that they may have ganged up on him through the years and made it very tough on the man. He tries to explain this to his mother, tries to resist giving over to her martyred point of view, as he always has in the past. But she will hear nothing good said about his father; she is jealous of his sudden interest in his father and still wants him all to herself in order to compensate for the bitter failure of her marriage.

I saw this actress making a strong defense of her point of view, I believed the relationship with the husband and the past injuries she had sustained, but I saw little warmth, little expression of love for her son. "But I don't like children," said the actress, "and I have no maternal instinct at all; it's just not in me." I pointed out that in the classroom situation the actress was forever giving Kleenexes to fellow actors who needed them, had a supply of Band-Aids and aspirin and extra matches ready when anyone had need, was solicitous and kind and helpful to younger actors—indeed she was the den mother of the entire group. "Is that being maternal?" the actress asked, astonished. "But these are my peers!"

I pointed out that her "peers" were the same age as her son in THE SUBJECT WAS ROSES, that had the class been made up largely of ten-year-olds or sixteen-year-olds, she would probably have treated them in the same maternal way, that the maternal or paternal exists in all of us, frequently guised so we can express it to gain our own satisfactions. I am constantly surprised at how little actors know themselves, since I expect (inaccurately) actors to know themselves better than other human beings do. They should. They must deal in the immediate use of themselves in their work, all the time, all their lives through. But in truth, actors know themselves no better than the rest of us do; their own image of themselves is usually standing in the way of their acting, since it provides both *limitations* ("I have no maternal instincts") and *prejudices* ("I hate children. How can I ever express love for a child onstage?" or "I'm not queer. How could I ever imagine being in love with another man?"), both of which hamper freedom and expanded expression.

Every time an actress hears herself saying things like "I have no maternal instinct," she must closely examine such blithe prejudice to discover where it causes a limitation in her acting. Limitations can be dealt with. Substitutions sometimes work: if you hate little children, make the child into a teen-ager. If you're crazy about cats and dogs, that might work, although I'm suspicious of animal or plant substitutes for human beings. You can find other, more positive ways in which you express this kind of feeling of motherliness: giving caring advice to friends, mothering your fellow actors, helping strangers on the street, and so on. Such instincts are pretty universal and hard to kill; if we're set against them in the usual form they take, they pop out in some sublimated form. An actress need not change her prejudices or her personal life. You need not give up your dislike of children, but you can learn to overcome your prejudices by using them in a positive way in your work. To do that, you have to know what your prejudices and limitations are; your work on yourself starts with the confrontation of those idiosyncrasies. Once they are known, you can begin to use them to advantage in your acting. If they remain unknown, you are victimized by them.

Guidepost 6: Discoveries

You have all undoubtedly had an experience similar to this one: A married couple have been together some ten or fifteen years. The wife serves the husband grapefruit, and he says, "Why are we having grapefruit again? I hate grapefruit." And the wife replies in astonishment, "I though you loved grapefruit. Why, Frank, you've always loved grapefruit." If human beings who have been together every day for years can make that kind of discovery about each other, then how can an actor do less?

Every scene is filled with discoveries, things that happen for the first time. No matter how many times it has happened in the past, there is something new about this experience, this moment. Each of the many scenes between the constantly bickering George and Martha in WHO'S AFRAID OF VIRGINIA WOOLF would be boring and tiresome if the actors did not find what is new, what is different, what is particularly at stake in the scene. Acting is a whole series of discoveries.

The discoveries may be about the other character, or about oneself, or about someone who is offstage, or about the situation now or the situation as it existed ten years ago and how that affects the now. The more discoveries you make in a scene—the less you rely on "we do this every day"—the more interesting your scene will be. It's hard to bring vitality and life to routine, but they are difficult to escape when you have the excitement of discoveries. Take nothing for granted; make an emotional discovery as often as you can find one in every scene.

Ask youself: What is new?

A FAR COUNTRY *by* HENRY DENKER

This play is about Freud's relationship with a female patient Elizabeth whose rigid physical disability he suspects has an emotional cause that is so psychological in origin that if he could only get her to face it and come to terms with it, she could be cured. She and numerous doctors are, of course, convinced the disease is physical in origin.

The actor doing Freud was very authoritative; we could believe he was an estimable doctor. We could see him probing, pouncing on her, forcing her to seek the truth, but since there was no obvious warmth written into the scene, the actor was cold in his authority. Could we have cast a cold actor to hold the stage the entire evening? Our play would fail.

MS   Did you look for warmth?

FREUD   I didn't find any in the writing.

MS   Then the actor's job is to add it.

F   But I don't find doctors, particularly psychiatrists, very warm people!

MS   We're not doing an average session with an average patient and an average psychiatrist, are we? We're doing this man Freud's whole life in one scene. You understand that? The stage compresses experience, which is why opposites are so essential. Freud was loved, even worshipped by many people, so he must have had his warm side, or he'd simply have been admired and not loved. So how would you find warmth in the scene?

F   By thinking of opposites. Since I chose to be very objective, very psychiatrist-like, if I'd thought of opposites, I'd have found some way to be unlike a psychiatrist.

MS   What way?

F   If I'm a pioneer in this kind of work, my investment in this woman would be much more personal. If I can finally get her to respond to my treatment, I can prove a whole new theory. It would make me famous; it would make me right.

MS How would this new personal involvement be expressed?

F By getting excited when she responds well, by getting depressed or angry when she rejects me. By *needing* her responses, not in just a clinical way like with another patient, but desperately needing to reach *her*. Ah, I must *communicate* with her, so I have to watch her carefully to see how she's responding to what I am doing.

MS So instead of being detached, you are really intensely involved with her?

F Ah, yes! My role that I try to play is that of objective doctor, but underneath I am terribly needful of her. If she resists my treatment, I am a failure. If she goes along with it and responds fully, I can prove to the world that my psychiatric theories are true. So every discovery I make about her is of utmost importance to me.

MS Do you see the mistake you made? You didn't determine what was really at stake for you and make it a matter of life-and-death importance. You treated her just like one more patient. Those everyday choices don't work for an audition. Therefore the discoveries you made were cut and dried instead of excitingly new to you.

F If I'd known the entire play, that would have been apparent to me. But just to be handed this piece of a scene . . .

MS I sympathize with that problem. But you've got to make important life-and-death choices every time you read! You can't afford these everyday choices, or someone else will get the part. If you had decided this was the most important patient in your life, then you would have cared, you would have found many different ways to get at her, instead of one dry, conventional, objective psychiatrist's noncommital way. And you would have been able to make a discovery about every revelation that came out of that woman on the couch there.

F Then, you are saying that everything that happens in the scene is predicated on our making an *important* choice of what we are fighting for?

MS   Right. In this case you should have chosen: If I don't get this woman to react in the way I think she should, my whole career is at stake. That would have made you immensely sensitive to every word she spoke. Therefore the discoveries you made would have been important ones instead of everyday ones. It's those everyday choices actors make that are their undoing. Let us ask your patient some questions. Elizabeth, what are you fighting for in the scene?

ELIZABETH   I resent this implication that my disability is caused by some mental quirk, some madness in me. I'm fighting to convince him that it is indeed a physical impairment over which I have no control.

MS   What is the opposite of that?

E   Maybe he is right. Maybe it is all in my mind.

MS   Yes. I didn't see that in the scene.

E   But I don't see that in the writing.

MS   It's in the subtext.

E   I don't understand. What is the subtext?

MS   What is going on underneath the text. For example, if on the day your husband dies, you are buying a pair of gloves, the subtext of his death would greatly affect the way you felt, even if the action of buying gloves is ostensibly everyday. But nothing of the subtext is ever going to occur in a scene unless you, the actor, put it there.

E   Why would I want this psychiatrist to be right?

MS   Because then you might be cured. You might walk again, so you could lead a normal life.

E   Ah, I see. Yes. I see that I didn't chose to make the opposite as being of equal strength to my original choice.

MS   You must. Then you could have made important discoveries.

E   I see that now. I could have discovered that my difficult relationships with my father and mother could have contributed to my disability. I could have discovered that this strange new doctor was the one person who might really have helped me. I could have suspected something was wrong about myself.

MS   Instead you chose to resist every discovery possible in the scene in favor of supporting the dialogue.

E   Then one literally supplies the opposites, even if you don't see them anywhere in the writing?

MS   Right. They are the subtext.

E   Why aren't they in the scene, why aren't they clearly written?

MS   A good play is a mirror of the way human beings behave. The actor's job is to provide what is *underneath* the behavior of human beings.

E   And an actor can only do that by finding the opposites, which are discoveries that the character, in her own prejudices, may be denying.

MS   Right. That is why opposites are so important: one must take the risk of putting them into the scene. What is written is obvious. It's what is under the obvious that makes for interesting acting.

E   What is the difference between a discovery and an event?

MS   The more important you make a discovery, the more it becomes an event.

As you see from this scene, it is the actor's job to look for opposites to what is written. Neither actor in this case picked a great *need* in him or herself for the partner. When there is need, there is warmth generated. We see many cold readings, in which the actors are uncaring and ungiving, but since the actors have made cold choices, how is there going to be warmth in the scene?

If this actor's Freud had needed encouragement, response, approval from his patient, the warmth would have been there. He would not have lacked authority, for the conflict would have existed between the authority figure and the human being in need of encouragement. Both can exist; one need not eliminate the other. Thus conflict can be generated in the character, but in this actor's choices there was none.

This actress's Elizabeth accepted everything Freud said. She was unquestioning, unneedful of warmth. She seemed to understand every word that was said to her. She never asked for more than the writing indicated to her. If she had put herself into the situation, however, instead of merely accepting the written Elizabeth, naturally she would have desired warmth, affection, and approval from her doctor, and thus she would have protested the singular cold authority she was getting. A more interesting actress would have appeared, one who protested as well as accepted, one who had fire as well as saintliness. This woman made many revelations to the doctor, yet the actress never added her own questionings: What does he make of what I've just told him? Doesn't that convince him? If not, what is he thinking? Does he think I'm a liar? Why doesn't he say something clear to me? I don't want to be here, it was never my idea to come here, I'll leave! No, perhaps I'll stay; he's curious, perhaps there is something to what he's doing.

Actors need to work from real-life situations, not literary or character concepts. Most often the discoveries aren't written on the surface of the script; the actor has to dig in the subtext to find them. They come out of the actor's own life questions.

Guidepost 7: Communication and Competition

Communication

Most people take the process of communication for granted but really don't know what it is. Acting is supremely a task of communication. It is not enough for the actor to *feel*, if that feeling is not being communicated.

When a scene fails, an actor will frequently say to me, "But I felt it!" If that feeling is not being communicated to the other character onstage, nothing has happened. Of course, it must occur internally, but to have it existing secretly inside of you isn't dramatic or active until you *need* to have it felt by the other character.

Communication is a circle, not a one-way street. You hear people say in life, "But I told him!" as if telling *at* somebody were sufficient. If he hasn't received what you've told him, there is no communication. It takes *two* to communicate: the sender and the receiver. The receiver has to acknowledge the message by sending a reply back to the sender, thus completing the circle before a communication has taken place.

This imposes a constant obligation on the part of the sender to (1) make sure his message is clear and (2) check that the receiver has received it. And an obligation on the part of the receiver to (1) make sure he's heard the message and is able to *duplicate* it and (2) let the sender know he's received the message. Without the process of duplication there is no communication.

Communication's not easy. We all tend to be lazy, thinking, "Well, I said it and it's his fault if he doesn't get it." Every time we think that, the communication fails. It's hard work communicating. Particularly because we must constantly play both roles, the sender and the receiver. Many of us prefer to play only one role, convinced we're not up to the schizophrenic activity of being two. But two we must be if communication is to take place onstage.

Think of it as a circle: what you send out, you must get back. Until the circle is completed, you can't go on to the next step in the communication process.

Let us call each act of communication a cycle. When the circle is not completed, people get stuck in that particular cycle. Either they go over it again and again, or they close up; either way they are not open to hearing the next cycle of communication. If the sender goes blithely on, he has left the receiver behind; he's now talking to himself. Soon he'll blame the receiver for not listening; or the receiver will say, "I don't know what you're talking about," and hostility will result. A collision, head on, because communication has not taken place.

Worse, there may be no overt declaration from either the sender or the receiver that the communication has broken down, and each will assume he has understood. On the basis of misunderstanding, they will plunge ahead into further and further difficulties, blames, misconceptions—all of which will inevitably lead to hostility.

Communication is much more than the exchanging of words.

Ask yourself: Am I sending out and getting back feelings, or am I just talking?

The most successful actors are those who are able to project what they are feeling to someone else. This sending of feeling to another person becomes so strong that it is projected to an audience.

The goal of communication is duplication. You want the other person to think as you do, to repeat what you have just said, to feel what you feel, to agree with you. Of course one does not always achieve this goal—other people are reluctant to listen and even more loath to agree—but this is the need and the motivation that is behind every communication.

We often fail to communicate in life; we tend to talk *at* people instead of *to* them. We tend to hide feelings and expect others to dig them out of us. Plays are not concerned with this everyday behavior of ours, but with the unusual moments in a person's life when his need to communicate is at its greatest. These are the needs the actor must furnish.

Receiving the feelings of another is even harder than sending out feelings of your own. It requires sensitivity, a heightened awareness of another person. It requires the investment of real caring; otherwise why will you undertake the formidable task of opening yourself up to true communication?

Receiving requires that we be open, willing. How can we receive if we are closed up? Being open is an act of both generosity and selfishness: generous in opening yourself up to receive another's needs; selfish in the greed of wanting to know another person, for there is power in knowing another.

There are occasions when we need to know another person, where it is difficult for us to live unless we do know them. There are opposite occasions in which we are willing to respond to another person's need to reveal himself to us.

When actors give me a selfless reason for an action in the play they are doing, I tell them to be suspicious. Few of us are Florence Nightingales. There is always a selfish reason why we are unselfish. I don't mean that people don't do generous acts, but in every generous act there is always *also* a selfish, personal need that is being answered.

It's important for an actor to remember this. Unselfish motivations lead to passive, saintly, and very dull acting. Only by a recognition of what you are fighting *for* can make your acting vivid, alive, memorable.

Communication is based on the need to be heard by your partner and the hope that what he hears from you will make a *difference* in his relationship with you.

Communication is the desire to change the person to whom you are communicating.

Competition

Every time I tell actors that all dramatic relationships are competitive, there's a lot of resistance. Somehow competition has a dirty connotation. No one wants to admit he is competitive in human relationships of love and friendship. But without competition between the characters, drama is dull indeed, since it feeds on conflict and dies with agreement.

There are two points of view an actor should imbue every scene:

1. I am right and you are wrong.
2. You should change from being the way you are to be what I think you should be.

No games are any fun unless the participants compete. Would you like to play tennis with someone who won't fight to win? He's no fun to play with. Would you like to play bridge with someone who's indifferent as to whether he takes a trick? He's a bore to play with. Life is a cabaret, my friends; you have to compete, or you aren't of any interest to anyone else.

We compete for everything: to tell the funniest story; to be considered the most truthful or sincere, the prettiest, the sexiest, the most reliable. We compete for room on the subway, for enough to eat, for jobs, for love, for affection, for friends, for lovers. There isn't anything for which we don't compete. *Competition is healthy.* Just as no game is worth the playing unless we compete, so no life activity is worth the doing unless we compete. Competition is life.

Yet most actors refuse to acknowledge this. They don't want to compete. They don't approve of the concept. And they are therefore not first-rate actors. The good actor is the one who competes, willingly, who *enjoys* competing.

The resistance to the concept of competition is enormous. In every class I teach, I find actors refusing to accept that competition is a part of every relationship. Evidently we are raised to refuse to acknowledge competition. We think it isn't nice. We frown upon it. Other people may do it, but they are not nice people; nice people like us do not compete. I have the devil's own work to try to persuade actors that they must compete, in every scene, or they'll fail. I say: "Competition is healthy." You can see skepticism on every face. They won't agree to that.

I find more resistance to this concept than to any other.

I hammer away at it: an actor must compete, or die.

Guidepost 8: Importance

Plays are written about the most important moments in people's lives, not about their everyday humdrumness. If they featured the humdrum, who would leave home to go see a play?

Yet actors seem fond of doing Everyday Life, congratulating themselves on their Truthfulness in doing so. The truth is not enough if it is neither dramatic nor interesting nor unique. We have lots of truth all day long, ground into us endlessly, usually someone else's truth, which they insist we know whether we want to or not. We have our own truths to face all the time, unattractive and unappealing, so that it takes every ounce of imagination to create some sort of dream to hold on to, however foolish, however unlikely, however hidden. People live for their dreams, not for the oppressivenss of truths.

Actors are also unaccountably fond of reducing all dramatic possibilities to the most Everyday Realities. They take a situation fraught with the potential for tension and iron it out until it is flat. Flat and controllable. They present this to you as The Truth, as Reality; then they wonder why it is of no interest to anyone. A tiny dust mote of real life, no more important than something swept under a bed. The truth is not enough for a play unless it is invested with sufficient emotion to make it important.

I suppose this ironing-out process, whereby the possibilities for drama in a situation are reduced so far they can be easily handled, comes from the inclination of most human beings to avoid trouble. Most people would walk a mile or sleep a week to avoid a confrontation. We are trained as children that the most admirable conduct is that which causes the least trouble, so most of us spend our lives avoiding the conflicts of which drama is made.

It's important for an actor to realize that what he must use in his acting is the opposite of what he has been trained in life to seek. Peacefulness and the avoidance of trouble won't help him in his acting. It is just the opposite he must seek.

Another factor that contributes to the flattening process is that actors, while well trained to search for the truth in their acting—a goal I heartily commend—make the mistake of equating it with what they see around them every day. The truth we seek in acting must be a highly selective truth, not an everyday, ordinary household variety. If what you present to us as an actor is everyday, no one will be very much interested in seeing it; after all, we see it every day. What an actor must look for in a play is something unusual. Something important.

You've watched people run for a subway: when they miss it and the door closes in their faces, they throw a fit, screaming and cursing and stamping their feet. The fact that there's another subway coming along in seven minutes doesn't dampen their conduct. Right now, at this moment, catching that subway is the most important thing in the world. Will you do less than that for a scene in a play?

My classes run longer than most (six to seven hours at a stretch), and so we have an intermission midway, when the actors can order coffee and have a break. Look at the faces when they are handed a black coffee if they ordered it with cream and sugar. Listen to the howls of dismay when they are given a doughnut if they ordered a Danish. Will you do less than this as your reaction to a situation in a play?

Important does not necessarily mean significant to others. It means emotionally important to you at this moment. We make trivial things important to us at the moment, even if a day later we will have forgotten them. Important things are made even more important to us. Don't choose less than the anguish of utter indignation when you miss a subway. Don't choose less than the heartrending howl when you are given black coffee.

Make the stakes in each scene as high as you can. Look for the maximum importance. Add importance. If you don't, no one will be listening to you.

EXAMPLE

BIRDBATH *by* LEONARD MELFI

BIRDBATH is a favorite play of Off-Off Broadway productions. There are only two characters; shy, fey, inhibited Velma and the handsome, disenchanted Frankie. They meet in a restaurant and Frankie asks her home with him. The writing seems to indicate that Frankie thinks she's a weirdo (which she is), that he gets as disenchanted by her as he does by everyone, that he fails to score with her and isn't even sure he wants to do so. There's something passive, introvertive and unwanting about Frankie that traps a lot of actors. I ask this actor some questions:

MS   Why did you ask her home?
FRANKIE   I felt sorry for her.
MS   So you're just doing a good deed?
F   Yeah.
MS   There's nothing in it for you.
F   Maybe I'll feel better because I helped out this poor kid.
MS   So you're Florence Nightingale? Always beware of choices that make you into the angelic, helpful nurse. Of course, we do things to help other people, but there's got to be something in it for us, too.
F   What could I want from this scrawny kid Velma? You mean I want to go to bed with her?
MS   Why not?
F   Jesus, I'm not that hard up.
MS   If you regard her as a dog, you'll never find a reason to desire her. Think hard. What would you want from her?
F   Maybe I want her to admire me.
MS   Okay. Why her? Why particularly Velma?
F   She happens to be there cleaning up the tables when I close up the restaurant for the night.

MS The choice of "happens to be there" is never a good one. It's circumstantial, it's not a strong choice, it never helps the actor. You've got to find a reason why you *chose* that person. You did ask her to come home with you, so you did choose her.

F I would choose her because she is hard up and she might make me feel like a real hot shot.

MS That's a very good reason. More.

F She might love me.

MS How much?

F (Surprised) Oh. She might love me more than any other girl would because she would appreciate me more, she'd consider herself so lucky to have me.

MS Very good. It's getting stronger for you. You've shown how she needs you. Now, what do you need her for?

F To make me feel better. To make me feel loved. Even to make me feel lovable. I'm at a kind of low point in my life —my writing hasn't gone well, I'm working in that lousy restaurant—she could make me feel better about myself. She would adore me, worship me, make me feel like a god again. She'd make me feel important. Maybe she could even get me writing again.

MS Could she help you in the writing?

F Yeah! She could have my pencils sharpened and make sure I have paper and carbon paper, she could sit real still darning my socks while I worked, she wouldn't be the restless type, expecting me to take her out dancing when I wanted to be home writing. She might be very supportive that way. She could type my manuscripts for me, and she could believe in me.

MS What do you have in common, you and she?

F Nothing.

MS Think again.

F What could I have in common with a poor lost creature like that? I'm handsome, I've had a lot of girls crazy about me; she's a pathetic, unattractive little virgin with no one in her life but her crazy mother and a brother that ran off and left her.

MS Did you say she was a poor lost creature?

F That's how I see her.

MS That's sort of how I see you, too, Frankie.

F You do?

MS You said yourself: You've got a lousy job working in a restaurant, you've got no bread, your writing isn't going well. You must be pretty lonely or you wouldn't invite this poor waif home. Sounds to me you got a lot in common.

F Well, if you put it that way.

MS Does putting it that way give you more of a relationship to work on?

F Sure, if we have a lot in common. I recognize in her a lot of things similar to me, only I feel better off than *she* is, don't I?

MS Sure.

F But that makes me the strong one, so I can reach out and help her. And then if I do, like I said, she can help me, encourage me to write, keep the place neat and tidy, do the shopping and cooking—then I'd have time to write. If she just wouldn't get in the way.

MS Don't you think you can lay down the law to her and get her to do things the way you want them done?

F Sure, sure, I could do that. She might be very helpful. More than those girls always wanting a new dress and want to go out to a new restaurant and go dancing and go to a show, using up all my hard-earned bread. Still . . .

MS Still what? Tell me.

F I'm not sure I'd want anyone to see me going out with such a plain jane. What if they found out I was living with her? I wouldn't feel so hot about that.

MS Is she really so plain? Take a good look at her. You could get her a much better looking dress. You could get her hair redone. Some makeup, a few touches here and there— you could really improve her a lot, couldn't you?

F Yes, I could. She doesn't have to look that frumpy. Maybe if she got some confidence . . . she could look pretty good. Still, she could never be beautiful.

MS She just might offer you a lot more than a beautiful girl.

F Possibly.

MS And ask a lot less.

F It might be a pretty good bargain. If I could fix her up . . .

MS You've seen the Hollywood movie where the plain girl who wears glasses and her hair up in a bun gets redone— she takes off her glasses and they make her up so suddenly she looks glamorous and beautiful. Why couldn't that fantasy be working for you here? You're Rex Harrison, she's Eliza Doolittle, you make her over and pass her off as a duchess at a grand ball.

F   Right! That's great. I could make her into a whole new person. No one would recognize her. Not even her mother.

MS   Fine. Now, what difference would having all this information do for you in the audition?

F   All this new information makes my interest in her now *important*. I was lackadaisical in the scene because I chose unimportant feelings, like being irritated and bored by her, but now I see all the exciting possibilities I could create in her. I could be imagining a future relationship with her that would change my life as well as hers. I could be working to get her to relax and trust me and let down her guards so we could really try things out. It could make an important difference for the rest of our lives. It could make the scene very alive for me. I'd like to try the reading again right now!

MS   If you will take away from this the lesson that you believed every negative choice in the script, that you operated out of boredom and indifference to your partner (which are the worst relationship choices an actor can make), and that if you ask these same questions of yourself about *every* scene you do, you could be just as eager to get up there and do the reading as you are now.

    Let me ask Velma some questions before you read again. What do you think of Frankie?

VELMA   He's one of the most attractive guys I've ever met.

MS   Why do you go home with him?

V   Because I'm afraid to go to my home.

MS   Why do you go home with him?

V   I thought I answered that? I didn't answer that. All right. Well, I go home with him because he asked me.

MS   No will of your own, eh?

V   Well, he seems kind and I've got nowhere better to go.

MS   That's a terrible reason to pick. You go to an attractive man's apartment late at night just because you've got nowhere better to go? What can come of that choice except a lackadaisical, dull, lifeless reading?

V   He doesn't seem like a very nice fellow from the way I read the scene.

MS   Then, you better find a way to make him nice.

V   I don't think I like him much. How can I think he's nice?

MS   That's exactly what I thought when I watched the scene. Here's a girl, lonely and shy, who's come to a man's apartment, but she could just as easily be walking in the park all by herself. He doesn't interest her at all. So why do you want me to watch the scene? When you're not interested in your partner, you're not very interesting to watch. If you're dull and uninteresting, why should I hire you?

v   You mean I've got to pretend I'm interested in him when the script says I'm not?

MS The script doesn't say you're not. You decided that.

v   The script says I'm afraid of sex. Every time he touches me, I ask him not to do that. I tell him he gets pretty mean when he drinks, I tell him he gets angry over nothing, I tell him he uses foul language, I ask him not to touch me.

MS True. All true. And is that all you see in the scene?

v   That's what I see.

MS You don't see that underneath those negative actions is a lonely girl longing for someone? Trying to find a way to get this man to like her? Being hurt by his cruelty, his language, his drinking, but being extremely attracted to him?

v   He doesn't seem attractive to me.

MS Which is exactly why you don't seem very attractive to us.

v   You mean if you're going to want to hire me, you should find me attractive?

MS I do mean that.

v   And that if I am not attracted to him, you're not going to be attracted to me?

MS I do mean that.

v   But that seems like a betrayal of the script.

MS I think BIRDBATH is about two lost and lonely people who are desperately looking for love. If you aren't looking for love, if you don't think you might find the love of your life in Frankie, if you can't create a fantasy of romance with this man, then how can I do the play with you?

v   How can I make that choice? The script clearly says I'm afraid of sex.

MS If you're afraid of sex, why do you come to his apartment?

v   To show him he can't pull any funny stuff with me.

MS Why do you pick that strange goal?

v   Because men think every time a girl is being friendly, it means they can lay her. They can't.

MS I see. So you're going to use this scene to make a platform for women's rights?

v   It's got nothing to do with women's rights. It's just the way men think, and it's got to be changed.

MS Do you intend to remain afraid of sex your entire life? You're never going to try to improve the situation?

V Sure. When I meet the right man.

MS Ah! At last. Why can't Frankie be the right man?

V Because I don't like him.

MS But if you did like him, then he could possibly be your fantasy of the right man?

V Sure. But I don't like him.

MS Which is more valuable for you to choose for the reading: that you like him or you don't like him?

V Hate is a very strong force in people.

MS But you hate your mother. Are you going to spend your entire time in a two-character play hating everyone?

V I see what you mean.

MS What are you going to do about it?

V I don't see any evidence that I could fall in love with Frankie. Not with *him*.

MS I do. I find great evidence in the script. So would you, *if you'd look for it*.

V You mean I got to turn every play into a love story?

MS Every play is about love. Sometimes it's about hate, which is the reverse. Hate happens when a person is deprived of love. That's why you hate your mother; you never had love from anyone. The more you are deprived of love, the more you are in need of it.

V I don't think that's what the play is about. I think these are two crazy mixed-up people who use each other. There's no real feeling between them.

MS Even if you were right—and you're not—who would want to see an entire play about such people, who have no more dimension than that? We want to see people who have dreams, aspirations, needs, wants. People with dimensions, not two shits you don't give a damn about.

V You mean I've always got to make positive choices like that?

MS In every scene. BIRDBATH proves my contention: The negatives are always written; you can't avoid them. The actor has to provide the positives. Look, you said yourself, it's written that you object to his drinking, his language, his disillusionment. But you have to provide the romantic reason why you're there in his apartment! That's the actor's job. Remember, you also say in this play that he is handsome, that your mother would adore him, that she'd be proud of you if she could see you with him, that he's very interesting and bright and intelligent.

v So I really dig him, huh?

MS Which choice gives you most mileage? Which gives you the most to work with?

v That I'm really interested in him, sure; that gives me the most to work with.

MS Then, always choose that. You won't be able to avoid the negatives; they're always written. That's why if you make a positive choice, that you have a real interest and attraction to your partner, you'll always use both sides of the scene. I'll get to know more about your emotional life because I'll see what you like as well as what you don't like, what you want as well as what you disapprove of, your dreams as well as the reality you have to contend with in the scene.

v How can I be interested in having a romance with this guy when this very morning over breakfast I murdered my mother?

MS You can choose that fact as a down, or you can use it as an up.

v I murdered my mother and I can use it as an *up*?

MS Sure.

v That's far out, man.

MS Not so far. Look at both sides: You've murdered your mother because you couldn't stand the torture of living with her anymore. She made your life one long painful wound. Of course, you feel guilt, but you also feel justification. That woman had it coming to her. Therefore you can feel free for the first time in your life. That must be what you feel, since for the first time in your life you go home with a man. That's an act of freedom, an act of choice.

v But wouldn't the guilt of killing my very own mother take over?

MS Do we like feeling guilt?

v No, I hate it. But we feel it.

MS And since we don't like feeling it, we try to do something about it. Guilt makes us feel bad, so we try to find someone to make us feel good. That's why you decide to go home with Frankie: maybe he'll make the guilt go away. Maybe he can help you when they discover the body. Maybe he'll stand by you through the trial. Maybe he'll fall in love with you and be waiting for you when you get out of jail. Maybe he'll help you find a lawyer who can argue your case for self-defense so brilliantly that you won't have to go to jail, and then you could have a life with him. If you were listening between the lines, you'd know that Frankie needs you every bit as much as you need him. You're in a terrible mess: you need love and help from someone. That's why you pick Frankie. With the hope you'll get help from him. With the hope he'll make it all right. With the hope that he will love you.

V   That's pretty big fantasy.

MS Exactly. That's what an actor needs to do a reading: a pretty big fantasy.

V   I'm a realist.

MS Maybe realists can't be actors. Maybe only people who believe in fantasies can be actors.

V   Ouch.

MS Besides, you aren't the realist you say you are. How could anyone call herself a realist and still want to be an actress? Wanting to be an actress is living in the biggest of all fantasylands! Right?

V   You're right.

M— No one, not even a realist like you, can live without a dream: a hope that something better is going to happen to you.

V   I dig.

MS If we didn't have dreams and fantasies that things would be better, that something wonderful is possible, we'd all be off the bridge long before now. What confounds me is: Why do actors so love to make the negative choice? Look how you fought like a tigress to hang onto your negative choices! And negative choices don't do you any good; they drown you, obliterate you; they keep any auditor from knowing who you are. They're only one side of you, and they're not the side that motivates your life! You are motivated by dreams, not negative realities. Reality creates the problems, dreams are how we deal with them. Dreams are why we stay alive. If you leave out your dreams, you leave out the very best part of you as a human being.

Guidepost 9: Find the Events

Actors frequently get so involved with character and feelings, with the subjective life of the character, that they forget about what is happening in the play. I call what happens in the play *the events*. One of the actor's chief tasks is to create the events of the play.

What are events? Events are of many natures. An event can be a change. That is the strongest kind of event. An event can be a confrontation—and for every confrontation there is always a result, a consequence for the actor to present. An even can be a climax, which is a major turning point in the lives of the characters.

Change can be overt or hidden, clear and outright and obvious, or subtle and obscure. Either way the actor must keep a sharp lookout for the changes in a scene, for there can be many. The more changes you create, the more alive the scene is, for every major change is accompanied by several minor changes along the route. Just as a plant changes every day of its journey through life from birth to death—you can almost see the daily changes in a plant—so does a human being change. Fine actors register these changes, which is what keeps us fascinated in them.

A play must move, it must progress, it cannot stand still. Events make a play progress; character or behavior alone will not do that. Something has to happen to move the narrative forward.

In many modern plays, the events are so hidden they are almost imperceptible. It is the actor's task to root them out, to make them happen, for the modern playwright is frequently reluctant to admit he needs events. Yet if the play has any worth at all, there are events, like roots of trees, hidden down there under the surface of the play waiting for the actor to grasp hold of them and make them *happen* in the play.

An actor must ask himself: "What happens in this scene? What are the changes?" And then he must work to create those happenings and changes. He must not accept that nothing happens or that there is no change; something must happen, some change must be effected. If the playwright fails to provide it, then the actor must.

There are events that involve one character in a scene and not another; or the same event may involve all the characters, but their reactions to and evaluations of the event may be totally different. Yes, an event can involve one character, while another is totally unaware of it. But the most valuable events for an actor to seek are those that involve the awareness of all the characters.

Actors get so wrapped up in the creation of behavior that they frequently overlook what happens in the scene. Behavior is not enough. An actor stands still, merely *demonstrating* behavior, unless he couples it with the forward progressive motion that comes with the creation of events. If you make nothing happen in a scene, it soon dies.

Events can be psychological, such as the exchange of power between two characters. The more that is made into an *action* by the actors, the more effective the reading. It is entirely up to the actors how action-filled an event may be.

In NIGHT MUST FALL by Emlyn Williams, when Olivia returns to the house to stumble over the body of her employer and then confronts Danny with this murder, the scene can become more exposition of the reasons why Danny was led to murder. By insisting that the changes in the scene be *events that are shared with Olivia*, requiring her awareness and acknowledgment, Danny can create a whole series of fascinating actions. It's up to the actor to make the choice. Clearly, actions are always more interesting than mere talk. The same material, with no change in the writing, can become frought with suspense and movement if the actor chooses to insist on playing actions that require relationship to occur.

In GYPSY by Arthur Laurents, which has just about the best written book of any musical I've ever worked on, the scenes between Herbie and Rose are filled with changes and progressions in their relationship. The more discoveries the actors make about each other, the more fascinating the scenes become. Events are discoveries that are made important to the point where changes in the relationship are effected. When Herbie finally "discovers" a fact he has unconsciously known all along, that Rose will always give him second place to her ambitions for her children, there is a major change in the relationship. That is why they eventually part. But if each discovery along the journey is made eventful, if he threatens to split each time he finds that out about her, then the reading can be suspenseful and unexpected.

That fascinating scene in Samuel Beckett's ENDGAME between Clov and Hamm in which Clov threatens to build a raft and sail away, leaving Hamm there on the beach alone for the rest of eternity, can be pretty flat unless the actors compete with each other to insist on the importance of their events. Hamm decries Clov for finding a flea on himself, which may herald the beginnings all over again of the human race; Clov resents Hamm's position of superiority in their relationship (because of age? experience? greater knowledge and sophistication?) and therefore finds ways to threaten to leave him. Events and importance go hand in hand. If you estimate that an event has only minor importance, the scene will be lifeless and lacking in drama. It's once again up to the actor to bring importance to the decisions about creating events.

The questioning of Mrs. Robinson by Benjamin in THE GRADUATE can be tedious unless the actors create events of importance. Benjamin's discovery that Mrs. Robinson sleeps on the other side of the house in a different room from her husband can be an event of major importance to him. It's up to the actor. When Benjamin starts inquiring about her daughter, Mrs. Robinson can sluff it off as of no interest to her, or it can become an important event. It's up to the actress.

The constant conflicts between the brother and sister in HOME FREE by Lanford Wilson can be just a series of domestic squabbles, but if the actors make them important in their efforts to determine who will win their fight to stay alive, *in her way* or *in his way*, then these events will carry the play along in a pattern of suspenseful offensive and defensive maneuvers that are eventful and revealing. Unimportant events reveal little.

EXAMPLE

THE ZOO STORY *by* EDWARD ALBEE

The opening scene between Peter, the older, settled, East Side man who is sitting on a park bench reading *Time* magazine, and Jerry, the young West-Sider who accosts him, taunts him, compliments him, and interests him is a scene that can be virtually eventless in the wrong hands yet rich in exciting events if the actors choose to find them. Two actors have just finished the reading.

MS   What would you do if a strange man came up to you in the park this way, Peter?

PETER   Me? I'd leave.

MS   What made you stay in the scene?

P   It says to.

MS   Not a very good reason.

P   I suppose I think he'll go away if I just wait it out.

MS   Not a very good reason.

P   He sounds crazy to me.

MS   Maybe that's exactly why he does interest you.

P   Do crazy people interest you?

MS   They must. I work with actors all the time.

P   Actors aren't dangerous.

MS Some are. Actors have threatened to kill me, or beat me up, because I wouldn't give them a reading. And those who don't threaten overtly, sure give me looks that could kill.

P But you're getting paid for it.

MS I *choose* to do it, don't I?

P Yes.

MS Just as you choose to stay seated on the park bench talking to Jerry, don't you?

P I guess so.

MS Don't guess. Don't be half-hearted. Say yes and mean it. That's why so many half-hearted auditions happen; because *you* don't commit yourself.

P But why would I want to talk to such a nut? Someone so hostile?

MS Opposites. Clearly you do not like his hostility, but there's something about him you do like. What?

P I don't know. I honestly don't know.

MS Describe your life to me.

P I'm married, I've got a good job at a publisher's, I've got two children—both girls—and a parakeet, and I lead a very good life. I'm fairly successful, and I live at a good address.

MS So you lead a very conventional life.

P Yes. You could say that.

MS Is Jerry conventional?

P No, he's not.

MS You've heard that opposites attract?

P You mean I like him because he's unconventional? Oh, I see! Because he's not at all like me. I'm fed up with my safe life; that's why I had to get out of the house, that's why I'm sitting in the park, that's why I talk to this strange guy.

MS Good. What are you looking for?

P A change. An adventure. Something different. And Jerry sure is different, all right. That's very interesting. The conventional side of me keeps threatening to leave, to hide from Jerry; the other side of me, the fantasy side of me, is curious about him and wants to reveal me to him.

MS Now do you see why the scene was so eventless?

P Yes. Instead of wanting to know Jerry, I chose that I didn't want to know him. If I were curious about him, the scene could be a whole series of discoveries I make about him, our differences, the contrast between my way of life and his. Every time we have a conflict, it could be an event. Every time I make a discovery about him—or me—it could be an event.

MS   Every time you make a negative choice about the relationship in a scene, you cut yourself off from finding the events.
You remain withdrawn. You may occasionally express hostility, but that's about it. You're not open for experience.

P   You mean that all the negatives are written in the lines, like
"Go away," "Leave me alone," "None of your business,"
and all my reluctance to reveal myself; but since I eventually do reveal a lot about myself, I must want to, right? So
I should have found the reason why I want to talk to this
man.

MS   Everything is possible if you say yes to the relationship.
Now, Jerry, why do you choose Peter to talk to?

JERRY   He's the only one in the park.

MS   Nonsense. In Central Park? You say you've walked for
blocks. And you haven't seen anyone in the park on such a
nice day?

J   Bad choice. So the park is full of people.

MS   More useful choice. Now, why do you pick Peter?

J   Because he happens to be sitting there when I get tired of
walking.

MS   Terrible choice. Accidental choices are never useful. Pick a
good reason for wanting to talk to him, to him alone, not to
someone else.

J   He looks nice.

MS   A bit tepid. Try harder. What does he look like?

J   He looks successful. He's got a good job. He looks intelligent.

MS   What do you want from him?

J   I want him to kill me.

MS   That's the end of the play. Do you want to play that now?

J   Yes. I think it's underneath everything I do in this play.

MS   Okay. Very interesting. In what way?

J   If I pick him as the one to kill me, then I have to watch him
very carefully and learn a lot about him in order to know
how to get him to kill me. Also, I don't want him to know
that's my intention, so I have to game-play in order to hide
that from him so he'll never suspect what I'm up to.

MS   Excellent. Now tell me why you picked Peter.

J   Because he's such an East Side type. I'm a West Side type;
they never accept me on the East Side. I resent his af-
fluence, his easy way of living, his adjusted, successful life;
whereas mine is always maladjusted, unsuccessful, unhappy. I want to get even with people like him, so Peter is

a good symbol of those people who've got it made. If I can turn him into a murderer, then I get back at all those people. So my motive is revenge.

MS   THE ZOO STORY is one of the most powerful pictures of revenge at work. Where does love come into it?

J   If I can get Peter to like me, then when he kills me, he'll feel terrible and guilty about it, which is why half of the time I pick on him and half the time I woo him, I flatter him, I express real interest in him, and I like him.

MS   You said the love came in because you want him to love you. Do you love him?

J   That's the irony. In the course of the play I get to like him very much, so even though I do get him to kill me and thus I do get to execute my revenge, after it's over I tell him to run away so no one will ever know he did it. So I let him off the hook because I learned to like him. The play ends with me doing an act of love, at last. I don't think I ever did a loving act before.

MS   How does all this—beautifully conceived, Jerry, to give you the maximum involvement to work with—create events in the section you just read?

J   Every time I score a point, when I reach him, that's an event. Sometimes I score by hurting him, and he resents me for it. Sometimes I score by flattering him, and he likes me for it. I get him very confused, but I keep him interested that way. See, he never knows what I may do next, so that way I keep him on the hook. I intrigue him. I have to keep score carefully. I've got to stay on my toes and learn to read him very intimately in order to know when I've scored or when he's indifferent to me. The scorekeeping is important. Each win or loss is an event. They add up to my getting him on my team little by little.

I wish I'd known all this when I went into the reading. I figured out a lot of it in advance, but the opposites weren't clear enough to me until I listened to you question Peter. Then I saw how creating the events—insisting that each win or loss is important and thus making an event out of each discovery I make about him, out of each time I hit home—will make our relationship very alive.

It's a great little play, isn't it? It's got everything: a fascinating relationship filled with opposites, a lot to fight for, importance in theme, a multitude of events. We play games with each other, and we each have a distinct role we play that has the opposite role in it, too. And it's filled with mystery and secret.

My moment before was that I've got this mysterious secret and I can hardly wait to find the right guy to spring it on. Won't he be surprised!

Guidepost 10: Place

Most readings take place on a bare stage, which is not the most useful environment for an actor. It's up to the actor to create a place, and it's well worth doing, for it will help him immeasurably in creating a reality for his reading. The immediate reality of a bare stage is a real down; an actor would do well to lift himself up, with a place of his own.

Since an actor is free to choose any place he wishes in which to do his reading—for it is he who provides the place in his imagination —it would be wisest for him to choose a place he knows well. A *real* place from his real life, so that he doesn't have to waste any time on being a set designer but will immediately know where the door is and where the sofa is and where the table and chair are. It doesn't matter that the person he is reading with (either the stage manager or another actor) is not using the same setting; it's what's useful for the actor that counts.

The physical nature of a place is only the beginning. The most important element is how you *feel* about the place. Take your own apartment: When you first look at it, you are uncertain: Should you rent this place, or should you not? Will you like it, or won't you? Can you afford it? Then you settle in, fix it up, make it suitable for you, and you like it a lot. Install a lover, and when he leaves, you'll hate the place you liked before. All the same place, but how you feel about it changes depending on the emotional events that take place there.

Once you have chosen the place, once you see it clearly in physical terms, then you must look for how you feel about it. The feeling is most important. That is what will elevate your use of place into emotional value.

Let me use some examples of the importance of place:

GOLDEN BOY by Clifford Odets has magical love scenes between the two young people that take place on a park bench overlooking Riverside Drive, with a view of the river, the George Washington

Bridge, and the cars whizzing by below. Not only are these elements sometimes referred to in the script, but the entire *rhythm* of the scene depends on that odd habit we have when seated in such a place of being affected by these outside elements because we can't take our eyes off them. The scenes are beautifully written to accommodate that reality. Yet I constantly see actors struggle with the rhythm and emotional meaning of the scene *because they fail to use the place*. I don't think these scenes can be accomplished without *seeing* the cars, the river, and the bridge and *using* what these elements do to the emotional longings of Joe Bonaparte and Lorna. They're in love and they shouldn't be because it will be a betrayal of the man whom they are both deeply indebted to, so the use of the place is a means to deal with the pressure of the love that is pounding down on them.

In Elmer Rice's STREET SCENE the lovers have an important scene at the end of the play where they part because they are unable to overcome the dominant power of the city street on which they live. If they don't use the street, the scene becomes an abstract discussion. Indeed, this whole play needs to be imbued with an important emotional use of the place. When you are outdoors sitting on the stoop of a building, it's different from being in your living room, yet if you watch most actors read, you'd never know where they are *because they don't know*. I hasten to add: It's not important that the auditors see your use of place. It isn't being done for auditors, it's being done for your own sense of greater reality.

Emlyn Williams's NIGHT MUST FALL takes place in the home of an elderly, hypochondriacal wealthy lady. Danny, the bellhop from the neighboring inn, resents her having that place: Why does she get to live there in comfort and wealth when he deserves much more to have it? The struggle over place is an important undertone to the entire relationship in the play. As Danny begins more and more to take over the place, ruling it and Mrs. Bramston, her secretary, Olivia, is amazed at his effrontery. She is resentful yet admiring of it. Hard for the actors to do without a sense of place.

NIGHT OF THE IGUANA by Tennessee Williams is a competitive struggle between Hannah and Maxine that takes place in Maxine's hotel. Since it is Maxine's place, she claims (and has) power over Hannah, who may be cultured but she can't pay the bill. The fight between the two ladies is brought to a climax because of the place where they find themselves. In another place, it might well be a different story, with the power on the other foot. Their high awareness of what the place means to them, does to them, is essential for a good reading of their scenes together in the play.

ORPHEUS DESCENDING takes place in Lady's store, so it gives her a power over Val that she wouldn't have if she had met him on his turf. The fact that her husband is dying upstairs affects both of them, so they need to *place* that husband. And why does Val seek refuge in this place rather than another place? Place will give the actor a lot to work with in this play, too.

THE HEIRESS takes place in Catherine's father's house in Washington Square, a place she detests and wants to flee. For her aunt it is a lovely and comforting refuge. Same place, two entirely different emotional attitudes toward it. For the father, the house is his kingdom and he is its ruler; for his daughter, it is a prison and she is his serf. He owns her as well as the house, so of course she rebels.

In the climactic scene in THE HEIRESS between Catherine and her aunt, Catherine thinks she is eloping that night with Morris and she'll never again have to set foot in this hated house on Washington Square and thus never again have to see her father. Each sound she hears she thinks is her fiancé coming to claim her. Once it is just a box blowing in the wind, other times it is a carriage going on to other destinations, sometimes it is nothing but her imagination. What is going on outside that window looking onto Washington Square is of utmost importance to both women: how can they read this scene without a strong sense of events that will occur in this place?

Velma in BIRDBATH comes to Frankie's place as a refuge from the world where murder takes place and jail awaits her. For Frankie, his place is his chance to show her who he is, and, of course it gives him the upper hand.

In Neil Simon's LAST OF THE RED HOT LOVERS, the lover himself, Barney, is caught in the embarrassment of having assignations in his mother's apartment while she's away at work. Each of the three ladies finds his choice of the place for a tryst to be rather bizarre, so for all the characters the use of place gives them a lot to play with.

Questions for the actor to ask: Where does this take place? How can I get mileage out of using the place in creating what I'm fighting for in this relationship? Geographical, literal place isn't important, except as to what emotional uses it can be put by the actor.

Guidepost 11: Game Playing and Role Playing

First let me explain that by game playing and role playing I don't mean insincere behavior. No matter how often I insist that game and role playing are real, actors persist in believing they are examples of pretense, make-believe, unreality, insincerity.

When we play games, it is for real; when we take on different roles, it is sincere conduct, for it is a way of *dealing with reality*, not of avoiding it.

Let me use an example: When I come to my classes, I play the role of teacher. The actors play the roles of students. If we meet at a cocktail party, we play the roles of peers: who can be the wittiest? We no longer observe the student-teacher roles but invest ourselves with new ones. We are the same people. We are not less real at a cocktail party, we are simply making a different adjustment to a different situation. We play the game.

When David Merrick calls me in to talk about casting a play for him, I don't play the role of teacher in that circumstance. No, indeed. Here I play the role of humble casting director. It is a different game; it has new rules; it requires me to play a different role. I am the same person, but in making my adjustment to a new situation I play a new role. So it goes in all the events of our lives. For each situation, we play a different role because it is a different game.

It helps an actor to ask himself in each scene: What is the game I am playing in this situaton? What role do I assume in order to best play this game? The answer depends on the circumstance: what people want from you, what you want from them, what you are offering, and what you expect. Ask what the stakes are, what you are playing for. But don't get the idea that you will therefore be unreal or insincere. Games are real; roles are necessary to deal with reality.

At the first class meeting, when I give the introductory lecture and explain these twelve guideposts, I use that physical and psychological circumstance to illustrate that we are there playing definite roles (teacher and students) in a game whose goal is the solving of an actor's great problem: how to get a job. We couldn't be engaged in anything more serious to us, and yet we play the roles and we observe the rules of the classroom game. It is of utmost importance to us, it is very real, we are all remarkably sincere.

Students ask me: What's the value of knowing this? An answer: Take the example of the relationship of son to father and mother. You may be willing to play the role of son because it is required of you, yet when the requirements set by your mother and father become too demanding, you want to cast aside the role of son and assert yourself in a new role: that of rebel. You become independent, and, of course, your parents protest this new role. They don't want a rebel; they want a son. You don't want to be just a son when you grow up; you want to be your individual. The result: conflict. Drama. Knowing the game and the roles you play helps you immeasurably to provoke conflict and to create drama.

If you play the role of son to your parents, you don't play that role with your girl friend: What would she want with a son? She wants a lover. So you play that role because it is the role she wants from you. But you don't play it insincerely, since you love her. It is a role and it is for real.

Every relationship we have demands a different role, in order to be successfully fulfilled. Every situation we are in is a game with different rules. All real. All meaningful to us. The rules of the game tell us how to act in the life situation, don't they? So they also tell actors how to "act."

EXAMPLE

SUDDENLY LAST SUMMER *by* TENNESSEE WILLIAMS

This is the famous Tennessee Williams play about a girl who is threatened with a lobotomy because she insists her homosexual cousin was eaten by a band of young children in a far-off foreign country. His mother is trying to silence Catherine so this story of cannibalism will never be known by the world, because in her eyes it would disgrace the memory of her beloved son. Catherine is brought to the garden by the nun who guards her at the asylum; she is to be interrogated by a young doctor who is trying to find out the truth.

In this scene between the nun and Catherine, the girl lights a cigarette because she is nervous about what is ahead of her. The nun forbids her to smoke, they disagree, harsh words are passed, Catherine finally puts the cigarette out in the upturned palm of the nun. I questioned the two actresses who have just read the scene:

MS How do you feel about this girl?

NUN She's clearly crazy. Anyone who would put her cigarette out in your upturned hand!

MS How do you feel about her?

N I think she's dangerous. I have to be very careful of her.

MS Is that all?

N I have to be very stern with her. She takes liberties the minute you're nice to her.

MS Then, shouldn't we see you being nice to her?

N I've been through this before with her.

MS Is it your job to be only a strict taskmaster? Shouldn't you also give her a chance? More than anyone else would?

N Oh. I see what you mean.

MS It seems to me you made a comment about what you think of nuns: that they're straightlaced, strict disciplinarians, starchy and uptight. That's all I saw.

N I think nuns are like that.

MS But if I want to give her more human qualities when I direct the play, where will I see them from what you did?

N I only played one thing?

MS You played your *judgment* of a nun. That isn't going to help me give some dimension to the role. A nun doesn't feel she's a disagreeable taskmaster. You've got to show opposites, not just one side.

N You mean I have to show love to this girl?

MS That's what I mean.

N How can you love someone who puts a lighted cigarette out on your hand?

MS That's the end of the scene, not the beginning. Actors fall into a trap of playing an event before it happens. You don't know she's going to burn your hand. If you choose to be very loving to her today, feeling sorry for what may happen to her about the lobotomy, then you can show many more sides to you; and the event when she burns your hand can come as a complete shock. If someone whom you love and trust burns you, isn't it more dramatic, more interesting, than if it's just what you expected? Doesn't it make it a richer scene?

N Yes. I see what you mean. Then I get to show many more emotions, because once she burns me, you get to see the strick disciplinarian, the uptight person, but before that you get to see me being loving and hopeful.

MS For you this is a scene about role playing. You have chosen to play the role of nun in your life work, not just to be mean, surely, but to give people the image of yourself as a warm, loving, devoted, giving person. That's what you'd be if you were doing your job well. If you are a mean tyrant, then you're not doing your job well but doing it badly. Always choose to do the role you play *well*; there's always room in the scene to show conflict, event, opposites. Actors too often choose to play their role badly.

N   You mean I must find opposites even in the job choice I have made in life.

MS   Every job requires that we play a role. A doctor has to play all-knowing healer, a nun's role is that of dedicated goodness and keeper of morality. But in addition to that, you should find a *personal* relationship with Catherine, different from with any other patient in the asylum where you work. Perhaps she reminds you of the daughter you never had, or of your sister. Something from your own life so that the stakes in the relationship are personal, caring, emotional. Then the effort to do your job on top of that emotional base gives you something much more interesting to play.

Let's find out what Catherine chose as her relationship to you.

CATHERINE   She's a very strict disciplinarian, and I always want to find a way to rebel against her because she just won't be human to me.

MS   That's an interesting choice. Do you like her?

C   Oh no.

MS   Why, oh why, do actors choose the negative answers? Wouldn't you get more complex emotional life out of choosing that yes, you do like her, so that you too are shocked when she won't let you have the cigarette, and you find you're putting it out in the hand of someone you liked and trusted who's suddenly turned into a martinet?

C   I see what you mean. You get to see more caring from me as well as the rebel in me.

MS   Right. Then the game of coaxing her into letting you have the cigarette is more personal, more playful, more fun. Then when you get furious at her and burn her, it's unexpected, sudden, much more dramatic. Neither you nor the nun nor the audience knows what's coming. Caring choices always lead to more unexpected behavior. The less predictable, the more interesting for the audience.

How do you feel about the doctor?

C He's blond. Blond people are blah.

MS Not a very helpful choice.

C That's how I feel about blond men.

MS Is that how you feel about Robert Redford?

C Oh no. He's dreamy.

MS Then make the doctor into Robert Redford. Make a positive choice.

C Oh, dear, there I go making the negative choice. I do feel that way about blond men, though, so I thought using something from my own life would be very real.

MS But you used a *generalization*. It's the *exceptions* that an actor should choose. It's what is exceptional that makes drama interesting, not everyday reality.

C If I make him Robert Redford, it would change the whole scene for me. I would want him to notice me, I would want him to know I'm telling the truth. Ah, I see, of course: the more personal I make my feeling for the doctor, the more important it is that he has got to believe me.

MS Good. What do you want the doctor to know about the Duelling Oaks scene?

C That some jerk misused me, and so I didn't trust anyone after that.

MS Were you in love with this "jerk"?

C Good lord, no.

MS Then if he meant nothing to you, how could he change the whole course of your life?

C He did?

MS You said you didn't trust anyone after your experience with him. You say in the play that something in you died, and after that you wrote of yourself in the third person as if the inside you were gone and you were watching someone else.

C That's right, that's right!

MS How could someone have that great effect on you if he was just a jerk and you didn't care about him?

C Maybe he raped me in the woods!

MS But you say in the script that you went to the Duelling Oaks section in the woods as if something mysterious were pulling you both there. You say you got out of the car first, you say you expected something wonderful to happen, and you were shocked when, after he took you home, he told you he couldn't see you anymore. That sounds to me like someone whose heart was broken, not someone who was raped.

C   You're right. Then, I went to the Duelling Oaks with this man because I thought I was going to have a great love affair with him? I'll be damned. I didn't realize that.

MS   Why not?

C   I don't know.

MS   Because you're not looking for romance. An actor must look for romance. Instead you all look for rape. Rape may be dramatic, but romance would be more so. When a man takes you to the woods and makes love to you and you think it's the most wonderful thing and you're going to spend the rest of your life with him, and then he dumps you, that's rape, isn't it? But it comes from feeling, from a romantic expectation, rather than cold-blooded indifference. Isn't that the more valuable choice for an actor to make? Clearly, in the script, you left the ballroom with this man and went to the forest Duelling Oaks because you expected romance. When you got hurt, you went back and made a scene on the ballroom floor; after that night your life changed completely. You had a traumatic injury, a romantic disappointment, which explains why you became putty in Sebastian's hands and his willing servant.

C   I see! By using your choice, the romantic one, I get to create romance *and* rape, so both things are put into the script rather than one, and I get to show more sides to my own feelings.

MS   Yes. By your choice that the man who took you to the Duelling Oaks is a jerk who raped you, all I got from that long section is a coldness from you, an indifference. Not only is that uninteresting to watch, but it tells me very little about you as an actress. Anyone can be cold: it's the warmth in a human being that interests us, the humor, the romantic expectations, the dreamer. All of that is possible in this script, and you left all of that out. The choices are up to you: You can make romantic choices or you can make cold choices. I've rarely seen cold choices pay off.

EXAMPLE

ENDGAME *by* SAMUEL BECKETT

Two actors were doing a scene from this rueful and very funny play portraying two men at the edge of the ocean. The blind one, who is also unable to move on his own, is "looking" out to sea, wondering if the human race is all over, if just these two are left. The ambulatory one knows how dependent on him the blind one is, so he taunts him with desertion: he will make a raft and sail away. Yet they have great need for each other and great fondness; after all, there is no one else left at the end of the world. I adore seeing actors do this scene, *if* they use some imagination and freedom. It marvelously ignites the creative spark in an actor if he'll let it. Many actors get up there and show how little they understand the scene; that's easy to do—who cares—they shouldn't be actors at all if they're not willing to find the humor in the world's end. But these two actors played the game marvelously: competing, fighting, needing each other. But no game is worth the candle unless the stakes are high. Few actors make the stakes high enough when they play their games; they make the mistake of assuming if it's a game, it doesn't mean much. Nonsense: a game must always have the highest possible life-and-death stakes.

Here are two men at the end of the world: what could literally be more life and death? Yet actors most often refuse to make the stakes important. What makes it important? Needing that other person or dying (murder, suicide, running away, being deserted). Needing independence from the need for the other person. Having to win, if this is your last day on earth. You can't take leave of the world a loser; there is just one final chance to win!

All game playing needs scorekeeping: The opponents need to keep track of who won and who lost each round in the fight, just as in a prizefight, in a tennis match, in any sport. It is important for you to acknowledge your wins and your losses so that your partner knows. Celebrate a win, cry over a loss. Let your loss stimulate you to make the next round a win. Let your loss be expressed in appreciation of your partner's expertise. Let your loss amuse you, hurt you, rev you up, push you down, spur you on. Let there be joy in your winning, real loss in your losing.

In ENDGAME the blind man says, "I need to take a pee." They are diverted by the possibility creation will start all over again; then the ambulatory one says, "What about that pee?" The blind one says, without moving from his stationary spot at the edge of the ocean, "I'm having it." Clearly the blind man wins this round. If it's done poker-faced, it's not as much fun as if the blind man celebrates his win over his walking-around friend. Register your win! Communicate your loss! Drama is conflict and communication.

The pleasure of playing the game is in the winning and the losing. Each round counts, for now; it may not even be remembered tomorrow, but for now it counts the most. Moment to moment winning matters to us; the more there is at stake in winning, the more fun and the more dramatic it is. If we don't care, we're not a good opponent; no one wants to play with us, and surely no one wants to sit and watch us play.

Play to win.

EXAMPLE

LOOT *by* JOE ORTON

When I worked on the Broadway casting of LOOT, which along with THE RUFFIAN ON THE STAIR is Joe Orton's best play, it was an appalling spectacle to watch how most American actors were totally unable to catch the tone. Actors rarely consider *the tone* of a play; they seem to regard all plays as naturalistic, all plays to have been written by Eugene O'Neill. Let us try to define *tone* for actors, which is the equivalent of the key to a piece of music. In which tone is the play written?

I am always reluctant to use the word *style* because it immediately seems to connote artificiality to actors, who prance around the stage, mincing and curtseying as if they'd suddenly been loosed from a road company of MARAT/SADE or from Bellevue. But we all recognize tone in life: it comes through adjustment to the level of game playing that has been established by the leaders of the game. Remember: game playing doesn't mean being unreal or artificial; it means getting into the spirit of what is going on and finding out how to fight for what you want in these particular circumstances. People do it all the time in life: they don't act in theatre lobbies the way they do at baseball games, they don't conduct themselves at a cocktail party the way they do at a Rolling Stones concert. So why should tone, the manner of behavior necessary in order to play the right game at the right time in the right place, be so hard for actors to discern?

Because they don't look for it. Because it's a concept that seems not to have passed through their pretty little heads. Because they regard it as something the English would do, not a straightforward American trait. Americans would do well to get over the mystique of being straightforward; it leads to a lack of dimension and awareness of how human beings really behave. Actors are led up the creek by this insistence that all is what it seems to be and that we don't play games because we're straightforward and games are deceitful. Games are not deceitful; they are the ways we deal with different situations.

I think THE RUFFIAN ON THE STAIR is one of the funniest plays ever written, with LOOT a close second. I wouldn't sneeze at EN-TERTAINING MR. SLOANE, also by Orton, either. But if you watch American actors struggle with auditioning for and performing these plays, you would think they had no sense of humor—or sense of tone. The game in LOOT is basically simple (once you catch on to the root, all games are simple): I can be more outrageous than you about my love for money, and I will do anything to get it.

Note what is in that simple statement:

1. I am fighting to have money because then I can have love.

2. I will kill for it (importance).

3. Do you mean you will kill for it, too? (discovery).

4. I'm just a simple girl (man) trying to get along in the world (role playing), but I'm really very bright underneath and I just act dumb.

5. Of course, I'm sexually attracted to others (in a perverse way, of course), but I know I'll never get anywhere with them unless I have loot.

6. Anything you can do, I can do better (Irving Berlin and Ethel Merman knew that; you'd think every apple-pie American would, too).

7. I'm witty and funny, but you're not (competition).

8. I have many secrets, and some I'll tell you and some I won't (Joe Orton is filled with mystery and secret, which is why his plays are such fun).

9. The events are found in one-upmanship (most actors read Orton as if he were totally eventless, so no wonder they don't know what's going on).

10. Place is important because someone owns the place and someone else wants it (look at LOOT and MR. SLOANE and the stranger who comes into Joycie's home in RUFFIAN). So competition comes into every single guidepost in an Orton play, another reason why they are so vivid: the people never stop competing.

11. One of their major competitions is: I'm more refined than you are. Since they are all ruffians, greedy vulgarians, this claim makes their competing for refinement very funny.

12. Perversity is the keynote: I do everything the opposite of everyone else. (Opposites abide in Orton; of course, they would in the work of a great comic writer, since opposites are the cornerstone of comedy.)

The people of Joe Orton will go to any length to get what they want: the more outrageous, the more they roll up their sleeves and dive right in. If American actors would only take this risk of wallowing in the outrageous while insisting they alone are sane, they might be able to discover the *tone*. The stakes in Joe Orton are literally life and death (someone always gets it: Grandfather is viciously killed in SLOANE, mother's corpse is hanging upside down in the closet and her coffin stuffed with loot in LOOT, the stranger's brother is run down and murdered by the hero's van in RUFFIAN, Joycie's beloved goldfish is killed at the curtain of RUFFIAN as a death of more significance than that of the stranger lying shot across the room).

American actors are not lacking in humor. If they persist hard enough—resistant though they are (because humor is too frivolous and Acting Is a Very Serious Business)—they'll find it. But *wit* does seem beyond all but a mere handful of American actors. Ask them what wit is, and most can't even define it. Since Shakespeare is full of wit, you'd think that would give them a clue; but Shakespeare gives them a clue to nothing, since all that concerns them when they perform him is The Beauty of the Verse. (I see whole productions of Shakespeare in which I can't follow the plot or determine the basic relationships because neither the actors nor the director ever gave those essential elements a single thought.) In modern plays wit occurs in Philip Barry's THE PHILADELPHIA STORY and T. S. Eliot's THE COCKTAIL PARTY and in some of Edward Albee and some of John Osborne, but since wit is intellectual, it's at a low ebb in most American playwriting. No wonder actors don't know what it is, since they've been raised on television, where the lowest common denominator is what determines what's funny and where people don't laugh at laugh lines, machines do. Wit is verbal and we're a nonverbal country; mumbling is our way of life. Wit is the taking of pleasure in words, in the way things are phrased; a witty person can say things in a more astute and sparkling way than a rival can say them. Wit is a highly polished competitive game, but since it's intellectual (a dirty word, to be eschewed at any cost) and requires the use of the mind, it's in very short supply.

A pity. Plays like THE IMPORTANCE OF BEING ERNEST can never be written in this antiwit, antistyle, anti-intellectual soil. A witty play is held to be anti-American.

How can actors act them when they are never exposed to them?

Guidepost 12: Mystery and Secret

In every lecture I give to explain the twelve guideposts I find the concept of mystery and secret the most difficult to explain satisfactorily. The concept is mysterious, too!

Let me put it this way: After you've done all the eleven guideposts in your preparation for your audition, then add to it what you *don't* know.

When I say this, a look of enormous skepticism comes over the faces in the class. "This fool has been telling us for three hours all the things we need to know, and now he says do what you don't know? That's our trouble: We're forever doing what we don't know at an audition."

But the most fascinating acting always has a quality of mystery to us. Garbo, Brando, Olivier, Davis, Guinness—these actors provide us with a dazzling array of answers (they all do the eleven guideposts thoroughly every time they perform), but then they add that quality we cannot explain, that exploration in relationships of what is wondered at but not answered, perhaps cannot be answered.

Think of some of the questions man has pondered since the beginning of his time on earth: What is love? Is there a god? Is there life after death? No matter how much science finds out, we never do know the answers to those questions, do we? They eternally remain mysteries to us. So it is with any relationship you create: No matter how much we know about the other person, there is always something going on in that other heart and that other head that we don't know but can only ponder. And no matter how we explain ourselves to someone else, no matter how open we are, there is always still something inexplicable, something hidden and unknown in us, too.

I am suggesting you add to your audition this wonderment about the other person. I am suggesting you add, too, the wonderment about what is going on inside of you. These are feelings, mysterious feelings, that cannot be verbalized and cannot be explained. But they can be felt and therefore they can be added to your audition.

EXAMPLE

THE CHILDREN'S HOUR *by* LILLIAN HELLMAN

In the final scene Martha comes to Karen, once she has learned that Karen's fiancé has deserted her, to confess that her love for

Karen is what others have said it is. Karen deals with this confession by insisting it isn't true. Every actress tends to assume that Martha feels guilty and makes her confession in order to deal with her guilt and that Karen is innocent of any such lesbian tendencies toward Martha.

But explore the mystery in the scene: Where is it written that Karen doesn't feel any sexual feelings for Martha? Because she doesn't say so? Perhaps they exist in her subconscious, and she doesn't admit to them. Perhaps this time she wonders if she does have such feelings. Perhaps she does wonder what it would be like to go to bed with Martha. Or she wonders why Martha can have such feelings toward her if she doesn't have any toward Martha? An actress can explore all of these mysteries, not merely the *no* of the scene (No, I don't feel any sexual longings for you). Again: the possibilities of yes are always more interesting to act than the certainty of no.

Explore the mystery of why Martha decides to tell Karen at this moment that she loves her. It has something to do with Karen's fiancé leaving her. Evidently that frees Martha to hope that the fiancé left because he suspected something sexual had been going on between the two women. Is he therefore possibly right? Dare Martha now hope that Karen may feel the same way about her? Since what motivates people is the hope that their dream will come true, of course Martha hopes that Karen's answer will be yes and that they can go upstairs to bed instead of Martha going up alone to suicide. A good example of why the actress should choose to play the possibility of the dream coming true. THE THREE SISTERS is not about three girls who don't get to Moscow, it's about three girls who dream of getting to Moscow and are determined to do it. THE CHILDREN'S HOUR is about Martha's dream of love from Karen. Both plays end in tragedy because the answer is no, but a good actress does not play the end during the journey, she instead plays the dream. The dream is that the answer will be yes, that she will get what she wants.

Don't play the end of the play before you get there. Play to win. Play to get what you're fighting for. No one in all this world plays to lose. Not even the self-destructs.

What is a secret? There are many variations:

You can have a secret that you really don't want anyone to know. I suppose that might be termed a true secret: one that you never tell and never want anyone to know. (Usually there's an exception to any well-kept secret, which is one of the fascinating things about secrets: sooner or later you tell *someone*. Human beings can't seem to bear keeping a secret totally to themselves, not forever.)

You can have a secret and want the other person to know you have a secret, even though you won't tell what it is.

You can have a secret that you want the other person to know you have, so they'll ask you what it is; and when they coax you fully enough, you'll finally tell.

We have insatiable curiosity about other people's secrets; we almost always want to know what they are.

We find ourselves mysterious. We cannot explain our own conduct at times. We ask, "Why did I do that?" and explore the secret in ourselves and ask others to explore it, too.

Oh, secrets come in many forms. I suggest you add that to your acting. Just as they exist in life in their myriad ways.

EXAMPLE

THE GRADUATE *by* CHARLES WEBB

Almost everyone knows the film version of THE GRADUATE and can remember the scene in the hotel room when Benjamin, who is just out of college and having an affair with a woman his parents' age, asks Mrs. Robinson if they can get to know each other instead of just fornicating.

MS   Why do you want to talk to her, Benjamin?

BENJAMIN   Because the screwing is so lousy, I figure I'll jazz it up a little with some talk.

MS   If the screwing is so lousy, why do you see Mrs. Robinson repeatedly?

B   I'm bored. I've got nothing better to do.

MS   Terrible reason. Every time I hear an actor say, "I'm doing this because I've got nothing better to do," I know why the reading is lousy. What gives you more to work with: that the screwing with Mrs. Robinson is lousy, or that it's absolutely great?

B   I suppose if it were absolutely great, then I really would be interested in her and want to know more about her. That would give me a real involvement with her, wouldn't it? You told us always to seek a maximum involvement, but I thought, "Jesus, I can't be in love with this old bag."

MS   Don't you find Anne Bancroft an attractive woman?

B   Sure.

MS   Then, why think of Mrs. Robinson as an old bag?

She's older than you, true, but she's a very attractive woman. With a good body. And she knows a lot about sex, and she's giving you the best damn time in the sack you've ever had.

B   Okay. That would be interesting.

MS So with that basis, why do you want to talk to her?

B   If the screwing's so great, why bother to talk?

MS Okay, Ben. Come on. Answer your own question.

B   We have great sex. I have a good time, she has a good time—why do I want to talk? She never says anything. I don't know anything about her. Ah, I'm curious about her!

MS Good. Go on.

B   I want to know what makes her tick. Does she think the sex is as great as I do, or for her is it just another screw? Does she think I'm something special? I'd like to know if she thinks I'm really good. Right!

MS So we have mystery and secret. She hasn't said anything, and you want to know what she thinks. Of you. Of what the two of you are doing. Of what her family knows. Does her husband suspect? How does she get out of the house? Is she in love with you, or does she regard you as a mere serviceman?

B   Yeah. I would like to know the answer to all those questions.

MS And all of them come out of saying yes instead of no when you ask yourself if the sex is good with Mrs. Robinson.

B   Right.

MS So always give an affirmative answer. It gives you a hell of a lot more to work with. The negative is always written; you can put it in as an opposite. But *curiosity* about the human being you're screwing is pretty natural, particularly about Mrs. Robinson, who's a very mysterious creature, never saying anything about herself or her husband or her daughter or anyone. That's unusual conduct; it piques one's curiosity, doesn't it? It gives you a big chance to explore mystery and secret in the scene. What is Mrs. Robinson's secret? You need to know.

B   You know, when you asked me how the sex was between us, I hadn't even thought about it before we did the reading. I thought, Here's this broad I'm screwing, and in this scene I try to avoid having to screw her again, so I ask her a lot of silly questions that don't mean anything to me. But what you're telling me is if it's a scene full of questions I ask, the questions should mean something to me.

MS   Of course. If they don't mean anything to you, why should an audience sit there? For such a long scene where you ask a lot of questions, she evades, you persist. You must be interested; why else would you persist so much against her refusals?

B   Right. And I just remembered, every time she asks me if I want to stop the fucking, I say, "Oh no, no. I want to go on fucking you." So I must like it, or why would I want to go on?

You say every scene is about love, yet I don't love Mrs. Robinson and she doesn't love me. So how is it about love?

MS   It's about *making* love, isn't it?

B   It's about two people screwing.

MS   Synonyms. Making love, screwing, fucking. But more importantly, it's about a question: How come, if we're not in love, we're spending all this time together? It's about two people wanting love and settling for less. Eventually you leave her for love; you find the love with her daughter that you didn't find with her. Mrs. Robinson is one of those poor souls who has given up love and settled for the emptiness of mere sex. So this relationship is *about* love, isn't it?

B   It occurs to me now that one of the reasons I ask her all those questions is that I wonder if she is in love with me.

MRS. ROBINSON   Isn't that just like a man? Of course, I'm not in love with him. He's just a convenience for me. I use him; he gives me what I want.

MS   And all you want is sex?

MRS. R   That's all.

MS   You've got such a great life at home, you're in need of nothing else but a little screwing, right?

MRS. R   That remark takes me back a bit. I don't have a very good relationship with my husband; we only have sex twice a year, on his birthday and at Christmas—

if he remembers when Christmas is—but a lot of middle-aged couples are like that.

MS   Because a lot of couples are like that doesn't mean it's all right to have a loveless life. Looks like the middle-aged are seeking love just as vehemently as the young these days.

MRS. R   But that's not what I want. I don't want love.

MS   Why not?

MRS. R   I'm too disillusioned. I don't believe in it.

MS   What do you believe in?

MRS. R   Not much of anything.

MS   Come now, Mrs. Robinson. There must be some reason why you stay alive.

MRS. R   I believe in my daughter! She's the reason I stay alive.

MS   Good. And is she the reason you are so secretive with Benjamin?

MRS. R   Yes. I think so. I don't want him to have anything to do with her. I need sex, but I don't want it to touch or soil my daughter in any way because she is the only good, pure thing in my life.

MS   So you consider your sexual experiences with Benjamin dirty?

MRS. R   Sure. We're just two animals rooting around in that hotel bed. It's just plain animal fucking.

MS   Animals don't think sex is dirty; they just do it. If you're doing it like animals, why is it dirty?

MRS. R   Well, it's a highly unsuitable match. I'm old enough to be his mother!

MS   Is that why you picked him: because he's unsuitable?

MRS. R   I hadn't thought of that. I thought I picked him because he just happened to be there, but you say circumstantial choices aren't good ones. Yes, I think that's a very good reason for picking him: He's so unsuitable I can't possibly fall in love with him; no complications can ensue.

MS   So love is a consideration?

MRS. R   I don't want love as a complication.

MS   So it could happen?

MRS. R   Yes, I suppose it could happen. I want to guarantee it doesn't happen.

MS   And you pick Benjamin to ensure it doesn't happen?

MRS. R   Yes. He's a safe choice.

MS   Then, why are you so upset when he starts to date your daughter?

MRS. R   I don't want my daughter fooling around with the man I'm sleeping with!

MS   Why not? What difference does it make if you don't feel anything for him?

MRS. B   Because I feel something for *her*.

MS   But you say yourself that Ben is wonderful in bed. If you don't care anything about him, why can't she have him if she cares about him?

MRS. R   The picture of him making love to her after he's made love to me—that would be filthy.

MS   Oh, so it is the image of lovemaking that bothers you. It is about love jealousy?

MRS. R   No, no, no. It's the image of his putting his penis into me and then turning right around and putting it into my daughter. That's repulsive.

MS   Incest?

MRS. R   No. It makes me feel like a whore.

MS   But you are.

MRS. R   I am?

MS   You said there's no feeling involved, you're just doing it to get laid. You said you're doing it because it is dirty; that's what you like about it.

MRS. R   Because it's dirty is exactly why I don't want him doing it to my daughter. I don't want her life to be dirty and a mess the way mine is.

MS   Do you think you're unworthy of love?

MRS. R   I never thought of that. I suppose I do.

MS   So you lack love for yourself.

MRS. R   Yes.

MS   So you're afraid to let love come into the relationship because it would be a betrayal of your love for your daughter?

MRS. R   That's right. She is the most important thing to me.

MS   Most mothers are able to love their daughters and love a man as well.

MRS. R   Yes. Well . . . I have this feeling I can't.

MS   Why?

MRS. R   I'm afraid I'll get hurt.

MS   Now we're getting somewhere.

MRS. R   You mean, I might fall in love with Benjamin, but I'm trying to ensure that I won't by making him unworthy of loving? So then, it *is* a scene about love —about me trying to guarantee love won't come into the relationship I have with him.

MS   Very good. It's clear that in the scene you are hiding something, which is why you don't want to talk to him or answer his questions. The actress must provide what it is that Mrs. Robinson is hiding.

MRS. R   And you think what I'm hiding is a possible feeling for him?

MS   What else would be a stronger choice to make?

MRS. R   Perhaps you're right.

MS   I'm not asking you to make this choice instead of the desire to protect your daughter. I'm asking you to make this choice *in addition*. It gives a much stronger emotional basis for the choice you do want to make.

That is why I advocate saying yes to the question, Am I involved with this man? Say yes. In any scene. It gives you much more to work with, it deepens your emotional involvement in the relationship. All the things you picked will be in the scene, anyhow, because they're written. The choice I have been leading you to make is to add depth to the choices you had already made.

Why do actors resist the involvement of love? It can only help them, in every scene they ever do.

MRS. R   So my mystery and secret is that I mustn't let this boy know how I am starting to feel. I'm also surprised I feel this because I started out just wanting to get laid and now I'm getting involved—against my will. So I am also exploring the mystery in myself: Mrs. Robinson, how could this happen to you, staring to fall for someone your own daughter's age? So then I use the opposite: I tell myself I'm not falling for him, I forbid myself to feel anything for him, I discipline myself. But there it is: this longing for him, this feeling I can't live without him.

I don't want to be involved with him, but I am. Yes, that is a stronger choice. I picked indifference to him: I can get laid by anyone; if you're not willing, I'll go find someone else. But your choice enables me to play that game but with some dangerous real feelings at stake under it.

All good plays have mystery and secret for actors to explore. Hamlet's curiosity about his mother's remarriage is never really answered to his total satisfaction. Something in Gertrude eludes him. And Gertrude is perplexed over her son's odd conduct. What is the secret he is keeping from her? Why is he acting in this unexpected way? What does he want?

Sir Thomas More in A MAN FOR ALL SEASONS takes a high moral stand, one that most lesser mortals would not be able to take. This must surely puzzle the people around him. Why is Sir Thomas acting this way? Does he really mean it? Will he actually give up his life for a principle? It is a mystery within the man to be explored by everyone else in the play.

The character that Al Pacino played in DOG DAY AFTERNOON is in some ways almost as complex as Hamlet. He has a wife and children, whom he seems very caring about; yet he undertakes the robbery of a bank in order to provide funds for his male lover. What makes this man act this way? What is the secret of his mysterious life? You cannot take for granted nor predict the conduct of such a complex, contradictory character.

Eleanor and Henry are forever mysteries to each other in THE LION IN WINTER. They are constantly predicting each other's behavior, yet finding each other unpredictable. They insist they know each other, yet they never lose their fascination for each other because *there is always more to know*. The actors who play these two marvelous roles had best explore the mystery and secret of such a relationship.

Robert De Niro is wonderful at creating the mystery of a character's inner life. In NEW YORK, NEW YORK we never knew what facet he would reveal next: Was he an outright bastard, or was he a man struggling to keep love and a career? It's his use of this kind of character mystery that makes his acting so mesmerizing, because it is rich in contradiction and opposites, and he never stops exploring the mystery of the relationship in which he is involved.

3

Consistency

Consistency is the death of good acting.

4

Some Things an Actor Needs to Know

What to Do When the Reading Isn't Going Well

There are two actions an actor can take when he feels the reading is going so badly it's slipping away from him: Blame or give.

Don't wait for a moment in the script that is appropriate enough to justify one of these opposing actions, for that will be too late. *Do it now.* You're drowning; rescue yourself. All the motivation you need is the way you are feeling about the reading. You are most likely blaming yourself because it's going so badly. That turns you inward and makes you introspective and inactive and alone, so that you are retreating from the scene.

You need to find an action that will involve you with your partner, and you need to find it immediately. *Blame your partner!* It's her fault the scene is going wrong. Yes, yes, I know it may not literally be her fault at all and probably isn't. Yes, I know this is an irrational act, which is exactly why you should do it: it is emotional, it will at once involve you in a relationship again with your partner—and the reading will come to life. Use whatever words the script provides you at the moment of need to create an outburst of blame that will rock your partner off her feet.

Then, if you feel so bad about unleashing your wrath upon an innocent partner, follow it with a total, unexpected opposite: You can make up for your dreadful conduct of falsely blaming her by offering her your love. A lot of love. Take her in your arms, give her a passionate kiss. (The absurdity of that will also bring humor to the scene.)

Actors protest when I advocate this. "But it won't fit the scene," they say. "It's not written that way." During my years of watching actors failing at auditions, drowning before my very eyes, I have also seen them rescue themselves by such an action, grab the attention of the auditors, and make themselves interesting. Of course, that fits! And remember, once more, that it is more important at an audition to show the auditors the extent of your emotional equipment as an actor than to illustrate your understanding of the script. What could more vividly show your emotional life than an outburst of blame followed by a warm offering of love?

The reverse procedure will also work when a reading is going badly: offer a sudden outburst of loving, contrasted immediately with an equally intense outburst of blaming. Now will come the time when an actor will say to me: "I offered her love and she responded to it. What do I do now? I got what I wanted; how can I blame her?" Easy. Getting what you want can be turned into not getting what you want if you don't believe the person who is offering it to you is sincere. We've all been in situations in life when a lady says, "I love you," and we don't believe her. Or the *form* of love she is offering is not the kind we are asking for. After all, some people go to the divorce courts still loving each other. They could never find the *terms* of loving they could agree on.

The terms of loving. This is a highly important concept for an actor. Most scenes in plays (as in life) are negotiations of terms between two people, whether they are lovers or enemies. Attempts to come to some agreement whereby one can hold onto one's own and so can the other person. This is conflict. Conflict is drama.

Conflict interests us much more than agreement. There is little drama in agreement unless it is preceded by or followed by great disagreement. If you're not finding it in the reading, create it, right then and there on the spot. You'll create it by blaming or giving.

To Change Your Partner Is One of the Important Motivations

Whenever you can't find any other convincing motivation in the scene, pick the desire to change your partner.

The wish to change our friends, our family, our lovers, everyone who is meaningful to us, is paramount. Human beings want other people to be what they think they should be, rather than just what they are.

To change someone is a highly active motivation choice. "I love you, but I want to change you." "Let me show you what I think you should be." "Let me mold you, and we'll both be happy."

The *terms* of a relationship are different for each person. The conflict over terms can be expressed through the *specific* ways in which you want the other person to change.

Never deal with the desire to change another as an abstraction. You must make the changes you want very specific. "I want you to learn to like my mother" rather than "A family should get along." Or "I want a divorce unless you stop eating crackers in bed and unless you get home from work on time every night" rather than "Our marriage isn't going well."

This is frequently a difficult concept for actors because we are raised to think we respect the people we love too much to want to change them. It seems unattractive to want to change someone else, so we keep that information about our motives from ourselves. Most people keep this secret so successfully that they themselves don't know it.

The secret is an essential piece of knowledge for an actor. He cannot function on the stage or screen unless he does desire to change his partner.

BORN YESTERDAY is a good example. Paul, the intellectual reporter, is hired by the uncouth Brock, millionaire—successful business tycoon, to give some class to his mistress, Billie Dawn. Paul becomes quite smitten with Billie, but since he is hesitant, almost cool toward her, actors are puzzled about what choice to make in the scene. What is Paul fighting for? To change Billie Dawn, in many ways: (1) to change her morality so that she won't want to remain Brock's mistress; (2) to make her fall in love with him; (3) to make her aware and "educated" so that she'll be a proper and fitting mate for him. Billie wants to change Paul from a stuffed shirt to a regular fellow so that she'll feel comfortable with him. The more specific the changes the actors choose, the more effective the reading, but all the choices that make BORN YESTERDAY work are predicated on the characters' desires to change each other.

About Friendship

One of the most difficult scenes for actors to do in readings is the scene that involves two friends. It usually comes off lackluster, rather spiritless, lacking in conflict or energy. The reason, I think, is that actors conceive of friendship as nice, easygoing, relaxed, comfortable, trusting. Lovely idea, but not really useful to an actor because it takes away any strong drive, any element of what he's fighting for. The results are scenes that are low-keyed and of little dramatic value.

There is an element in friendship of paramount importance, and most actors leave it out. It will help them the most. That is competition.

A lot of actors roar their protest when I say friendship is competitive. They conceive of competition as not nice, as aggressive and unattractive. One would not compete with one's friends; that would be a dreadful state of affairs.

But we do compete with our friends. It's one of the major reasons we have friends: stimulation. You can't stimulate each other unless you compete. To see who plays the best game of tennis or golf, who is the wisest and wittiest, who can bake the best cookies, who has the nicest children, who lives on the best block. Competition is healthy, yet actors (as do most people) regard the word *competition* with horror, thinking it only connotes cutthroat business or aggressive countries at war with each other. Of course, competition can be aggressive and warlike, but it can also be a healthy stimulus, such as wanting to play tennis with a partner who is as good or better than we are.

Friendship is perhaps the only relationship of equality we have in our lives. We can't be equal with a lover or a husband or wife, we can't be equal with our parents, and we certainly can't be equal with our children. In those relationships we *strive* for equality because it is so difficult if not impossible to achieve. But in friendship we can achieve equality. We pick friends who are peers, most of the time, rather than people inferior or superior to us. They may have qualities that make us feel they are in some aspects superior (or inferior) to us, but for the most part, the friendship rests on a bedrock of equality. It is this very equality that enables us to compete in a situation where we feel the competition is all right. So all right, as a matter of fact, that most people don't realize they are competing.

If we didn't compete, there would be nothing to stimulate us to do a thing well. Why bake good cookies if it is not because they'll be compared to other cookies that are good? Why play a good game of golf unless it will be compared to someone else's game that is good? We don't like to do things we don't do well; we don't like failure; we like success. It wouldn't matter to us if we succeeded or failed if we didn't compete.

There is an acceptance in friendship that enables us to relax and *enjoy* competing. Friendships—good ones, true ones, basic ones— tend to last longer than most other relationships. It's because there is trust, freedom to compete, freedom to criticize and to receive criticism—freedom because we are accepted and therefore honesty is possible. No other relationship in our lives is likely to be as honest as our close friendships. No other relationship is able to relax into competitiveness that is accepted on both sides.

To compete is not necessarily to injure. We stimulate each other through competition; we force each other to grow, to become more aware, to try harder, to exert ourselves, to reach out for what we have not yet attained. On our own, shy and unstimulated, we well might not.

To be sure, some competition is fierce. The desire to win may be so great that we will at times walk over our own friends. Or a friend may prove such a disappointment, such a sap, that we feel called upon to tell him off. We are more likely to dump on a friend, knowing the friend will probably forgive us and allow us to go on being a friend—and will dump upon us in return. It is this element of the *dangerous*, of putting one's foot upon the ice, that actors too often leave out of scenes between friends. In friendship the trust is great, and the disappointment, because of great expectations, is even more likely to spur us to action. We'll pummel a friend even more readily than an enemy.

So an actor must look for this element of danger in any scene between friends. If it seems not to have been written there, invest the scene with danger of your own devising. Placidity never made an effective dramatic scene.

When an Actor Has to Say "What?"

Actors frequently misunderstand why a playwright has a character say "What?" They spend a great deal of wasted energy trying to justify "What?" as if the playwright meant that the character hadn't heard what the other character had said. No playwright will waste the time just in order to repeat the information; he has an *emotional*, not a factual, intention. You must always assume you have heard what is said and that you are not asking to have it repeated because you are deaf or inattentive. On the contrary, you are finding what you have heard either unbelievable or unacceptable.

"What?" means "I would like to know what the hell you meant by saying that!" Or it may be a ploy for time: having heard something confounding, you are throwing sand in the other character's eyes until you come up with another, smarter move.

How to Tell a Story

A story well told starts from a point of innocence. We don't tell how a story turns out at the beginning, we create suspense. We create reality by telling the story in the same sequence as it happened to us, that is, we start from a *point of innocence*, the point where we were innocent of what was going to happen and thought it was going to be a day or night like any other.

Example: The class is over; it is midnight. I clean up the classroom, put things away, turn out the lights, go down the stairs to the street, and lock the door behind me. I notice a man standing on the corner in a pose of elaborate casualness. I lock the door and start down the street, but in half a block I become aware that the casual man is following me. Is he following me or does he merely happen to be going my way? I stop, pretending to look in a store window; he stops. I turn the corner, even though it's out of my way; he turns the corner, too. I finally turn and confront him: "Are you following me?" He takes out a knife. Etc.

But I don't start the story by telling you a man took a knife to me last night. That would not be telling a story well, for it would not make you, the listener, relive it as I lived it, *from a point of innocence*, the point where I had no idea anything untoward was going to happen to me.

Tennessee Williams is filled with the telling of stories that start from the point of innocence; so are many other playwrights. (Eugene O'Neill, an artless if powerful playwright, tended to tell the end at the beginning, but an artful playwright tells it as it happens.) It is an important awareness for an actor.

SUDDENLY LAST SUMMER is one of the best examples of telling a story from the point of innocence. Study that Tennessee Williams play; you will learn a lot from it. The heroine in it, facing a lobotomy (if the doctor doesn't believe her version of her cousin's having been eaten by human beings), tells several long, complicated stories in the course of the play. The doctor has few lines, merely encouraging her, stimulating her, supporting her, urging her to go on with the incredible stories she has to tell.

HOME FREE by Lanford Wilson is a two-character play about a brother and sister who are also lovers, who pretend they are husband and wife. Many a story do they have to tell. The point of innocence is essential to the performing of this play.

THE PRIME OF MISS JEAN BRODIE contains a scene between Miss McKay, the headmistress, and Miss Brodie in which Miss McKay starts from a point of innocence. Instead of accusing Miss Brodie at once and asking for her resignation, she traps her with a whole series of little games and ploys designed to make Miss Brodie undo herself. The game of cat and mouse usually starts form a point of innocence: Me? I'm just a pussycat, I wouldn't eat a cute little mouse like you!

If a playwright spills the beans and tells the end at the beginning, you still employ the method by starting all over, by going back to the point of innocence as you were when the event began, so that your partner shares that beginning experience and then each step of the journey to the denouement.

Stage Directions Are Traps

For the purposes of auditions, stage directions should be largely ignored. Some are necessary, of course. If the stage direction says you take a gun out of your purse and shoot the man dead, that can hardly be ignored. But stick to the essential stage directions; all the rest are nonessential and can frequently lead you into a lot of trouble.

Disregard directions such as "She said weakly" or "Ignoring what is said to her" or "Indifferent" or any of those thousand and one *negative* stage directions playwrights are so fond of because they think it will make their script more dramatic—and because they are describing what they see in their fantasy life, whereas you have to act what you see in yours.

Don't obey stage directions blindly in auditions. Use them only when they are useful to you.

Transitions Are Fake

Transitions are a thing that only actors do; I never see people do them. In life we simply shift at once from one feeling to another, immediately. We don't stop to show someone else how we got from feeling A to feeling B; we just do it. That's what makes people so perplexing. We're always marveling at someone: How did she get from being in love with him to suddenly crying over her lost dog?

Give up transitions. That's something unfortunate drilled into actors in acting classes. It doesn't belong in an audition. It's unlifelike. It's tiresome. It's obvious. It's unnecessary. And it's time-consuming. It comes from a desire to show what hard work you've put into the preparation of your reading. Auditors don't want to see the wheels at work; they want to see the result. The result is a series of actions, not transitions.

The more immediate and unexpected your opposites, the more fascinating is what you are doing because it is fresh, yours, and unpredictable. A transition kills all that. It makes what's going to happen next predictable. Avoid transitions.

In the rehearsal period you may need to make conscious the process human beings go through to get from point A to point B. Then you'll have to figure out the transitions. But that's your rehearsal activity. No audience during a performance wants you to explain how you got from one feeling to another; they just want you to do it.

So do it.

If the Audition Is Going Badly, Should I Stop?

No. Never. You may lose your place—you'll find it again. You may drop the script—but you can pick it up and go on. Interesting things invariably happen when there's an accident at a reading. Let them happen. Losing your place isn't a cardinal sin. *It's not a performance*. The auditors don't demand their money back if you lose your place; they know it happens. All they expect is that you'll find your place again and go on.

No matter how awful the reading is, don't stop. If you stop and ask to be allowed to start at the beginning again, the auditors will expect some great miracle to happen. It rarely does. I hear the auditors say, "Why did she start over? I don't see anything different."

Instead of stopping if you feel it's ghastly, go into the blame-or-love routine: Blame your partner, give him hell; or kiss him and offer him loads of lovely love. Either action, however unsuited to the script you may think it is, will connect you with your partner, will create relationship, will renew what you're fighting for, and will interest the auditors in you. There's nothing to be gained by stopping, and everything to be gained if you take a big blame-or-love risk to rescue yourself.

Which mountain climber is more interesting: the one who crawls back down and starts over, or the one who nearly falls off the edge of the cliff but rescues himself and keeps on climbing?

Truth Isn't Enough If It Isn't Dramatic

Actors are very worried—rightfully so—about being truthful in their acting. The tendency is to prize truth even when it's a tiny, mundane, everyday truth. But that's not enough. What good is truth if it's dull and boring? Exciting truths can be truthful, too. Learn to prefer those.

I find actors are hesitant to make extravagant choices for fear they won't be truthful. I'd put my money on an audition in which there's a little risk taking, a little push and shove, if it's in the direction of something extreme, unusual, out of the ordinary. In our fantasy lives and in our dreams we all commit rape, murder, incest, and any number of grandiose and bizarre sexual activities. While they may frighten us in real life, they're still real, they do occur, and we all know these experiences even if we haven't literally experienced them. Use them. Don't stick to the everyday. If we see it every day, who will go pay money to see it?

Be Wary of Playing the End of the Scene

I once directed a production of my favorite play, THE SEA GULL. We had a run-through midway through the rehearsal period, and it was splendid. From that point on, the players went steadily downhill. Everyone began to play how things turned out, so what had been an engaging presentation of complex human behavior became a dirge. The cast virtually cried their way through the entire play. They knew the end was coming, and that's all they played. Be wary of that. May I once again use as my prime example another Chekhov play?

THE THREE SISTERS isn't a story about three sad sisters who never get to Moscow; it's about three lively girls who fight like hell to get there.

You Should Embrace Melodrama, Not Run Away from It

As well as avoiding overacting, actors are afraid of being melodramatic. If they suspect there is melodrama in a scene, they will suddenly read at low key, with stoic resignation masking any feeling. Actors seem to feel the way to deal with melodrama is to avoid emotion. That way no one can accuse them of being melodramatic. That is also the way they deal with the possibility they may be overacting. They don't act at all.

When I ask them why they seem underwater, floating in a wet limbo—when I ask why they didn't make a stronger demand in the scene—they tell me: "I didn't want to be melodramatic." Why not? Who gave melodrama a bad name? People are melodramatic in life every day.

All that melodramatic actions need in order to make them real is an opposite: your awareness that what you did is indeed melodramatic brings a self-deprecating humor into the scene. Then you go right on being melodramatic. Humor can make any outlandishness real because humor is awareness.

There are two opposing choices we make in life when we're melodramatic: We can get so caught up in it that we don't give a damn; our need is so strong that we just charge ahead, melodramatically. Or we can become aware of it and make fun of it. It's investing melodrama with belief that makes it work. If you decide it's melodramatic in order to withdraw from it, you can never fulfill it. Withdrawal is just another inhibited actor being uninteresting; the woods is full of 'em. Plunge in. Give us actors who are willing to take the risk.

Of course, melodrama is a risk. Do you think THE GODFATHER or LENNY or LAST TANGO IN PARIS could have ever happened if the creators had been afraid of melodrama?

There Are No Passive Characters

Actors are fond of categories. "This character is strong," "this character is weak," "this one is aggressive," "this one is passive." Character *qualities* are of no use to an actor in an audition. Such abstractions do not lead to performing an action; they merely get in the actor's way. Judgments of character may help in the rehearsal exploration, but they only hinder the audition.

Forget about weak or strong, aggressive or passive. There are no passive characters, there are no weak ones. There is winning and there is losing, but every actor must fight *for* something he wants and needs. If you are concerned about getting what you need, then you will never let preconceived judgments get in your way.

The Purpose of a Reading Is to Show Who You Are

But not to illustrate that you know what the scene means and that you could direct it. You're not at an audition to do the scene right, but to show the auditors who you are. Give yourself a chance. Worry less about the material and more about what you would do and feel if you were in that situation. The play gives you a situation; your job is to put yourself in it.

I've heard directors say, "That actor did the scene all wrong, but he was so interesting. Let's hire him." The director is going to rehearse the play to show you how to do it right, so doing it right is not your major concern at the reading.

I've also heard directors say, "That actor hasn't a clue as to what that scene's about. Who's next?"

So it is a chance you take if you use yourself in the play's situation rather than trying to fulfill character. Since in the thousands of auditions I have witnessed, I have seen 162 percent more who won through using themselves than who predicated their audition on character choices, I would say the odds were pretty strongly indicating where to place your bet.

There's An Exception to Every Suggestion Made in This Book

Of course. But exceptions prove the rule. Always take into account what's different. Use your imagination, your instincts. Rigidity is death in an actor's life.

Bursts of Anger and Regret After an Audition Are Significant Signs

Meaning that you repressed yourself during the reading.

In my classes it is frequent after an audition scene that an actor will burst into fury at himself or begin to give a lively, funny commentary on what happened during the reading. Why didn't he use that fury and humor in the reading? It would have been far more valuable there, where the auditors could have got the benefit of this life force at work. Actors are often more interesting in the discussion that follows the reading than they were onstage, proving that (1) they weren't using themselves, and (2) they have repressed energy that should have been shoved smack right into the reading itself.

No wonder most readings are gray in color and lifeless in spirit.

Self-blame turns inward. It's energy that goes inside and kills you. Out it pops after the reading. Blame your partner in the reading —instead of yourself; that's connection, that's a flow of energy and life toward another human being.

There's Only One Reason Why a Character Drinks

Playwrights often use heavy drinking or drunkenness in their scripts because it motivates a heightened dramatic effect. Drinking characters are frequently more colorful. Can you imagine George and Martha in WHO'S AFRAID OF VIRGINIA WOOLF without alcohol?

Actors have a lot of trouble dealing with drinking, particularly in auditions. They get overly concerned with the physical side, go into clichés of falling down drunk, incline toward stumbling and in-coherencey—none of which is of any dramatic value to them.

There is only one reason why anyone drinks in a play: to release inhibitions, to be able to say and do things he was normally afraid to do, too repressed to do, too considerate or cowardly to say, too po-lite or fearful to risk. Have a few drinks and all this can come pouring out, once the blocks are down and the dam has broken.

This is the only positive, the only useful, choice an actor can make in the audition. Every other choice is a down. Choosing any-thing else, the actor tends to overlook relationship in order to mum-ble and meander in a highly self-indulgent manner, with little emotional purpose or drive for the scene. The drinking becomes an all-consuming irrelevance.

On the other hand, using drink to release inhibitions, to take down the walls and blocks, enables the emotional life to flow toward achieving what one is fighting for. It takes away the censor that nor-mally stops us from going after what we need.

Actors tend to use drinking negatively. It's important to find the positive: allow drinking to heighten the emotional needs, to free you to express deeply-buried feelings. Not to escape from relationship, but to pursue it. Not to become vague and fuzzy about the world and whoever is in it with you, but *to seek confrontation*, to fight for what you want in ways normally denied you. Not to withdraw from your scene partner, but to seek, in a richer, more needful way, warmth, camaraderie, love.

Remembering Is Seeing

In every new class I ask a student, "Where were you on Sunday afternoon at three-thirty?" Almost invariably the actor will look away from me before he can answer; he must *see* where he was on Sunday at three-thirty, or he can't tell me. Acting is seeing. That's what images are: pictures of what did happen to us, pictures of what may happen to us in the future. We see our entire lives in images.

And what does that actor see when he can finally tell me where he was on Sunday at three-thirty? He sees himself in an environment with other people. We see everything that way: not an isolated closeup of a face, but a person in a specific environment. Don't try to see a face when you are using recall of someone; use the entire person in an entire place.

In monologue work, where actors have such trouble seeing their imaginary partners or seeing other imaginary people in the scene, it would help if they would see *an environment*. They should see people in a place doing an activity that is typical of them; they should not try to isolate faces. The screen, particularly television, has misled us into thinking we see in close-ups. We see in long shots.

Acting Is About What We Do, Not What We Should Do

Acting is predicated on the ways in which human beings behave, not the way they *should* behave. I think actors frequently confuse the two. Of course, we all feel we should not blame others unfairly or be revengeful or compete unmercifully, but people *do* those things. Acting is doing what people do. It is not a moral act.

Only Actors Keep Eternal Eye Contact

Actors are the only people on earth who stare into each other's eyes when they are talking to each other. The rest of us human beings tend to look at what we are talking about: we see images on our own personal, private TV screen. Watch people in life: the one who is listening watches the one who is talking; the one who is talking is busy *seeing images* and only checks with his partner from time to time to get response, encouragement, and approval and to make sure the partner is still on the journey.

Actors stare into each other's eyes to indicate they are having a relationship. It's phony. Eyes go out of focus when they look into other eyes for very long. Don't see eyes, see images.

Lesbians, Whores, and Gays Are People, Too

Actors are often thrown for a loop when they have to read for a lesbian, a whore, a gay, a pimp. They seem to think these folk are so different from the rest of us that their behavior has to be peculiar, jazzy, bizarre, outlandish, and, most particularly, beyond anything the actor has ever done or experienced. When they play a prostitute, they are fond of jutting out their hips, walking as if they had stones in their panties, slapping their handbags, and chewing gum. These are the outward clichés of a whore, not the realities.

I point out to actors that in the very class in which they sit, on one side of them may be a call girl and on the other side may be a lesbian or a homosexual. The outward behavior may be no different from anyone else's; it is the interior emotional life that is important to explore.

In life sometimes people do dress up and act the role they are playing. Some whores get a kick out of rebelling against staid society, so they rub the straight's face in their outlandish costumes and actions; some effeminate gays do their rebellion in the form of a grotesque takeoff of women; a pimp may dress in colorful, bizarre high fashion to prove how successful he is. But costuming isn't going to get you the role; pasting on outer behavior isn't going to convince the auditors as often as your creating a believable inner emotional life in a relationship of need. Most people who deviate from normal behavior keep it a secret, so they look and behave with little difference from the rest of the world.

In BUTTERFLIES ARE FREE the young man is blind. Actors are fond of giving their all to the blindness: they stare straight ahead (as if they had a stiff neck) and often act as if they had no idea where the sound is coming from when someone speaks to them (as if they were deaf), they bump into things, they fail to take into account that this young man prides himself on his adjustment to blindness and is so successful at compensating that the young woman who's falling in love with him doesn't know for a long time that he is blind. The actor is so busy with The Problem that he neglects the relationship and the fun of the game of flirting with the girl. For the Broadway production, so many actors let the blindness get in the way of expressing their emotional life and their humor that actors were told to ignore blindness completely in doing the readings.

In THE GLASS MENAGERIE, the actresses who read for Laura sometimes relate more strongly to their limping foot than to the Gentleman Caller. Add shyness to the limp, and you get actresses who audition with their heads under their arms; you can neither see nor hear them, so how can you cast them? With so many liabilities, Laura is a typical "trap" role, filled with negatives, unless you strongly determine what you are fighting *for*, rather than drowning in Laura's afflictions.

Gum Is Not a Characterization

Whenever I see an actor come onstage chewing gum, I know we're in for trouble. Actors think chewing gum takes them into another world and makes them into another person; they rely on the gum to do the work for them. It doesn't. Forget the gum. It doesn't create relationship, it doesn't create what you're fighting for, it's cheap and obvious. What it does do is irritate the auditors and give them one more impediment to seeing who you are.

Many actors think this brilliant concept—gum chewing—is innovative. I've got news for you: auditors get to see at least ten gum-chewers a week.

Revenge Is an Important Motivation

Actors rarely pick revenge as the goal they are fighting for, yet revenge is one of the most important motivations in human nature. When we are deeply hurt, we want to hurt back.

Evidently this is human behavior so unlikable that most people hide the evidence from themselves. They don't *know* they are acting out of a desire for revenge.

And so often revenge is an act of blindness, a striking out at the next person who comes into our life for the injuries visited upon us by the last person. "Blinded by emotion" goes the phrase, and so, literally, we are unaware that we are enacting revenge.

RED CROSS, Sam Shepard's fascinating play, is an example of this. The young man stays in a white house in the woods with a young girl; one presumes, if they are not married, they are having an affair. The girl rejects his needs and goes off to town, leaving him alone in the woods with his secret self-destruct, a fear of solitude, a need for confirmation. The maid comes in to change the beds. She is clearly attracted to the mysterious young man. He plays on this attraction, takes her through a fantasy experience of swimming together naked in the summer night, and then rejects her and hurts her. Actors have a hell of a time finding the reason why. "Revenge!" I point out. They look startled: "But what did the maid ever do to me?" "Nothing," I reply. "Then why," they ask, "would I injure her?" "You make her pay for what your girl did to you. We frequently make the innocent pay. The girl rejects your needs, so you turn around and reject the maid." Still actors look puzzled.

We are so anxious to think well of ourselves that we blind ourselves to the true behavior of human beings. If you're going to be an actor, you'll have to start exploring the intricate, hidden, and frequently unfair behavior that is caused by our need for revenge.

Revenge is frequently long-lived. A hurt visited upon us by a parent or a childhood friend is frequently not squared off until we are an adult. Most of us may consider revenge but drop the idea because it is unattractive or we get over being injured; but those short-range revenges, important as they are, aren't the only ones that motivate our behavior.

Many a self-made important executive is the result of being overlooked as a child. Many creative people are "getting back" at being considered untalented or uninteresting.

Some Hollywood star beauties are proving to the world they can be wanted, after a childhood of neglect and rejection (the classic, and typical, example is Marilyn Monroe). These are all acts of revenge. Keep in mind that all revenge is not harmful or destructive; frequently it is highly creative, an enormous life force driving people to prove their worth.

NIGHT MUST FALL is Emlyn Williams's study of a young man from the lower classes who resents being treated as a nobody. He considers himself clever, shrewd, and observant (and he is), so he commits murders to prove to "them" that they've underestimated him. He might have chosen to commit poems or music instead and thus have forced the world to admire him that way. Isn't all our creative work the achievement of revenge against the doubting Thomases who said we couldn't? There are always the dubious standing in the sidelines to say we can't achieve our ambitions. If we show them we can, we get our revenge.

Seduction Is a Phony Goal

"To seduce" is an artificial and untrue goal. I doubt if anyone says to himself, I'm going out and seduce someone tonight. I think *seduce* is a word we use about other people, not about ourselves. We may think, I'd like to go to bed with someone tonight (and in terms less polite), but the concept of seduction is not a true one to most human beings and not a useful one for an actor.

The kinds of terms an actor uses are important. If he uses "to seduce" as his goal, then his acting becomes nonemotional, manipulative, crass. If he uses the seeking of warmth and union with another human being, the result is something likable. After all, we do know almost any human being can act like a shit, but what we're looking for in most actors is likability, warmth, and feeling. Even in casting a villain, if we cast cleverly, we want someone who can fool other people into thinking he's sincere and a hero.

Take an example: the film THE APARTMENT (which became the musical PROMISES PROMISES). Fred MacMurray is an outright seducer in that setup, yet he has to convince the heroine—indeed a whole series of bright, attractive young ladies—that he adores her and her alone. He can't do this by acting the seductor but must act the sincere lonely man in need of love.

For even the seducers are seeking love. They guise it from themselves (and more contemporary people do it than ever before) and insist they just want to get laid, but they do want to be wanted, and that is wanting love, even if you have no intention of giving it. The actor is always better off making the choice, then, of seeking love rather than seduction.

If everyone needed to be an aggressive seducer to get over being a virgin, most of us would still be virgins.

A Maxim for Actors

Use what you know. Don't worry about what you don't know.

Many times at a reading an actor is given a scene to read; he doesn't know the play, doesn't know what scene precedes or comes after it, doesn't know the storyline or the rest of the characters. An actor tends to worry about all these things he doesn't know, instead of concentrating only on what he does know and working with that.

What you decide about the scene, if you create a real relationship and use the guideposts, will do you just fine for a reading.

Use what you know. Don't worry about what you don't know.

Avoid Hunking

Actors tend to play hunks instead of opposites. A hunk is a section of "I love you" followed by a section of "I resent you" followed by a hunk of "Go away, drop dead."

Playing opposites, instead of hunks, is to play Yes, No, Yes, No, Yes, No, instead of ten minutes of Yes followed by ten minutes of No. Opposites are much more interesting than hunking. Hunks become predictable; opposites are more surprising.

Also: Your action can be an opposite to your words. Saying "I hate you, go away," while you kiss someone.

Find extremities in the opposites: the further you go in one direction, the more likely you are to express the opposite instinctively.

If you play your opposites simultaneously, they cancel each other out and paralyze you. Play opposites at different moments.

How to Take Care of Yourself When a Physical Activity Is Required

Since an audition situation is never rehearsed, an actor cannot rely on the partner in the scene to accomplish a given physical activity. The partner does not intend to fail, but he may not notice the stage direction, may have his mind on other things, may conceive of the action as taking place at a different time from your concept—any number of reasons may occur so that the physical action you are waiting for doesn't happen. What to do?

It is always wisest to conceive of the physical action in terms of your reaction to it. You can receive a kiss even if it is not given; you can react to being slapped even if no one hits you.

Many's the reading I've seen where the actor waits to be slapped, the slap never happens, the actor is thrown, and the emotional validity of the scene disappears because the actor was *dependent* on the slap and went to pieces when it wasn't forthcoming. But if you receive having been slapped, the emotional life of the scene can continue. What is more important, a literal slap or what happens to you emotionally when you are slapped? Clearly the latter; and that you can accomplish by an emotional decision.

Recently I watched two actresses reading that delicious scene from Jean Anouilh's RING ROUND THE MOON, wherein the lower-class girl and the upper-class girl are having it out. In the scene, the upper-class girl steps on the train of the lower-class girl and rips her lovely dress; in the reading I saw the actress wait and wait for the other actress to step on her train. It never happened. The girl didn't react to it happening, so the rest of the scene made little sense; her emotional commitment to the scene disappeared; she lost the reality. Since there was no actual dress, no actual train, why did there have to be an actual stepping on it when the most that could have happened was a pantomine step anyway? She could have received that any time she chose. The moral: in an audition, always rip your own dress.

Shyness Is Wanting to Be Bold

Actors tend to create a shy person through the generality of being shy. The action of being shy is wanting not to be shy but to be confident, bold, aggressive. The shy person dreams of being the opposite of what he is. His entire effort is to overcome his shyness.

Shyness is most convincingly created through opposites: making a bold move and then being overcome with shyness because you are afraid you can't sustain the boldness.

A consistent shyness is dull, inactive, passive. A conflict between shyness and the desire to overcome it is active and interesting.

Make the active choice.

For example, Velma in BIRDBATH: she comes to Frankie's apartment hoping he will help her get over her shyness. Laura hopes for the same from the Gentleman Caller in THE GLASS MENAGERIE.

Choosing to Ignore Your Partner Is a Bad Choice

Playwrights are fond of putting "She ignores him" into stage directions. This is a trap for an actor in the audition. Ignoring your partner is another passive choice; it inactivates you.

Instead, find the active of ignore.

We ignore someone because we don't like what he says. That means we wish he would say something other than what we are hearing. That means we want him to change.

The active of ignoring is to want the other person in the scene to change: to stop being what he is and become what we want him to be.

Find out what you want your partner to change to, and make that your choice. Make it specific.

For example, THE GLASS MENAGERIE again. Laura seems to ignore her mother and brother in most of the play. The actress must make specific choices of what she wants from them and create in silent dialogue the communication of her needs to these two people who are closest to her. She should create the fantasies of how she wishes they would treat her, how they would change and give her what she needs from life.

It Is Important to Study the Other Character in the Scene

Most actors, I find, study their own role and pay very little attention to the other character in the scene. Great mistake. You must study the other character since what you are doing in the scene depends on what he is doing.

You'll find more answers about what you are doing in the scene if you ask questions about the goals and motivations of the other character:

What does he want?
Why does he want it from you?
What does he expect from you?
What is he fighting for and what has that to do with you?
What is his past relationship to you?
What game is he playing? What is his image of himself?
How does he conceive of his relationship to you?
What is the conflict between you? Think of his side.
Put yourself in his shoes.

The more you know about the feelings and wants and needs of the other character, the richer will be the relationship you create and the better the reading.

What Listening Is

Listening is not merely hearing, it is *receiving* the message that is being sent to you. Listening is reacting. Listening is being affected by what you hear. Listening is letting it land before you react. Listening is letting your reaction make a difference.

Listening is *active*. Too many actors make listening a passive process.

Listening is talking while you are being talked to, not out loud but creating *silent dialogue* that answers what is said to you. This is active. Active listening is answering. Here is your chance to write your own play because the silent dialogue is entirely up to you.

The more specific your silent dialogue answers, the better your listening.

What Should You Do When You Hate the Character You're Playing

First, it's important to admit you do hate the character. Actors think it's wrong to hate the character, so they keep this information from themselves. Bring it out in the open. Admit it: I hate this character. That's the beginning of being able to deal with the problem.

Because the problem must be dealt with, not minimized or overlooked. I find a mysterious thing: when an actor hates the character, there is usually a profoundly personal reason. Sometimes because it's revealing a trait the actor doesn't like in himself; or it re-creates a real-life relationship that is so uncomfortable the actor wants to run away rather than deal with it (hating is a way of running away). We rarely have such a strong reaction as hatred unless it involves us deeply.

Try to be specific about what you hate in the character. If you can give specific reasons (rather than generalities), you can deal with them specifically. What was a liability can turn into an asset.

Try to find out if you also dislike the other character in the relationship. You may find it is the relationship you dislike rather than the character. That will give you further specifics with which to work.

A curious fact, I find, is that actors get in trouble when they love the character, also. Their favorite role in their favorite play is sometimes the one for which they give the most unsuccessful readings.

What either hating or loving the character means is that the actor is blinded by a *generalized* feeling reaction. Break it down into specifics, and you can beat the problem.

Suggestion: Read again the section in Guidepost Two on Charlie I in A PALM TREE IN A ROSE GARDEN for a further example of this problem.

All Human Beings Love to Suffer

One of the greatest competitions between human beings is about who has suffered the most:

1. I have suffered more than you have;
2. I have suffered more than anyone ever has;
3. You'll never know how much I've suffered, but you could at least try;
4. Let me tell you the extent of my suffering (you'll never believe it);
5. My childhood was total suffering, my wife doesn't understand me, I'm too sensitive, my trouble is I'm too truthful. Etc.

The reason people love to suffer is that it makes them right.

The reason people love to suffer is that it proves how deeply they feel; what profound caverns of emotion exist beneath that brave, smiling surface!

People fight hard to prove the extent of their suffering. They feel no one is listening. (And, most of the time, they're right. We human beings are incredibly self-absorbed.)

In making his competitive choices for any scene, an actor must always keep in mind how much we all suffer and how hard it is to prove.

Study LUV, Murray Schisgal's very funny play, which has the truest scenes of competitive suffering. Note particularly the section on the bridge where Ellen and Milt (or is it Harry?) compete over who had the most tragic childhood. "I was raped by two boys on Parsons Boulevard . . . I was raised by an uncle who was an alcoholic . . . I never got any presents on my birthday." The extremities presented may seem farcical, but they are also real. Compete. If you don't, you'll suffer alone. What's the good of suffering if no one else knows?

What Fear Is

Fear is what we don't know. The solution is to know what it is you are afraid of; then you can deal with it.

An example: A close friend of mine cannot go into his own apartment in the dark. He unlocks the door, stands uncertainly in the hallway while he listens, and then reaches in with one hand and switches on the living room light. He stands in the hallway, peering into his own living room. When he has carefully checked every corner from hallway vantage, he slowly enters, leaving the door opened behind him. Gradually he thus makes his way into the kitchen, the hallway, the dining area, the bedroom, the outdoor terrace. He looks under the furniture, under the bed, into closets, behind chests of drawers—anywhere someone might conceivably be hiding. With a sigh of relief, at last he is able to close the front door behind him, locking the four bolts and the fox lock and the chain and the police lock. It was years before I discovered that this terrifying fear came from a childhood experience. He was raised in a Catholic home where there was intense conflict between mother and father but no solution such as divorce. The parents left him alone frequently with a sadistic baby-sitter who would promptly lock him in a closet, then turn off all the lights and hide after unlocking the closet door. The child was forbidden to come out of the closet until a given signal, then he was forced to crawl out into the darkened apartment, knowing he would be leaped upon somewhere in his travels by the baby-sitter.

One time when we were walking in the country night, my friend let out a scream when a branch touched him in the face as it was suddenly moved by the wind. I realized then that his fears were at fingertip edge, ready to explode at the least accidental trigger. A lot of actors are like that. They scream inside, filled with horror at the sadistic audition situation that might accidentally touch a branch across the face.

I tell this story to illustrate what fear is: We fear what we don't know. Turn the lights on what we don't know so that we can see and therefore know, and we allay fear. Most of the time we find we fear what *isn't* there. About 99 percent of the time. When we do find a burglar hiding in the closet, our fears are indeed justified, but we have something tangible to deal with. We can hit him over the head with a chair, or we can run away. We can faint, so he can run away. We can ask, "What are you doing here?" and he can say, "I was looking for a collar button I lost ten years ago in this very closet." But most of the time our fears are groundless: we don't know why we are afraid.

Through the years, I have found most actors are terrified of the audition. They don't know why. It is a nameless, unspecified terror. The classes I have taught have for the first time given actors *specific ways* in which to function in a terror-filled situation, so the terror has disappeared. The actor becomes concerned with how to function, rather than whether or not he can. He becomes concerned with the elements of the scene that is his task to fulfill rather than worry about whether the auditors like him. He focuses on expressing his emotional commitment to the elements of the scene rather than try to please the nebulous desires of the auditors, desires that he does not know and has no way of understanding (so why should he be concerned with them?). In that direction of worrying about the unknown, fearing what might be in the minds of his enemy, in that direction resides the paralysis of fear.

Grant that the auditors have problems and uncertainties and prejudices, but since the actor has no clear way of knowing what those are, he is best left focusing on what he can accomplish rather than on what *might* be expected of him. Turn the lights on the audition instead of cowering in the dark closet. Learn to function, instead of being prey to your undefined fears.

Yes, I know these Norman Vincent Peale concepts are easy to say and hard to live by. Think of fear as being in the dark, and *learn* to turn on the lights. It isn't easy; no one promised you a rose garden when you decided to be an actor. It's going to be hard work all along the way.

Try to define what it is you're afraid of. List the elements. If you define what you fear, you might just be able to deal with it. Leave it an abstraction (which is what fear is), and you are lost. Pin it to the mat. There is something you can do about the fear of auditions: you can learn specific actions to deal with it.

Keep asking yourself: What exactly do I fear? The more specific your answer, the more you can deal with it.

Be specific.
Fear is a generality.
Be specific.

Actors Should React on the Line, Not in Between

Many actors are fond of reacting between lines, in those glorious and so often unnecessary pauses that they stick in between each line. So it goes in this unnatural rhythmic procession: line, react; line, react; line, react.

In life we are reacting with what we say while we say it. We don't separate our words and our feelings. Only actors do that.

Do it like life: React with the lines, not separate from them.

Accents Are Not Usually a Good Choice

Unless required. Find out: Ask the auditors if they want an accent in the scene before you go to all the trouble of creating one.

Some fortunate actors find accents very easy; some find it difficult. If an accent is required for the scene, best have a go at it, explaining that it will get better with time. If you're really lousy with accents, go work with someone who knows, and listen to records that contain the accent. And remember that it's the *music* of an accent that is important, not the way a particular word or letter is pronounced. No use saying *cawn't* in an English accent if the rhythm of the scene is totally American. Two suggestions:

1. Talk in the accent in your everyday life. Call up friends and talk to them in it, go shopping and talk to strangers in it. It's more important that you get used to the rhythm and music than to labor on the particular scene you are going to read, which will make it stilted and self-conscious. No matter how crazy the rest of the world may regard you, talk only in that accent for the time you have prior to the audition.

2. Don't let the accent become so primary that the reading becomes an exercise in doing an accent. Keep well in mind that you are apt to forget what you are fighting for and all your other goals when the accent is troublesome to you. Whenever there's an accent, be certain to *renew* your emotional goals in the scene often.

Two experiences:

When I was looking for an actress to replace Joan Plowright opposite Angela Lansbury in the Broadway production of A TASTE OF HONEY, the very best reading was given by an American actress with pronounced New York speech. I asked her to go home to work on the accent and then come back to read again. Three times she came in to read, and each time she was unable to replace her New York speech with an English equivalent. It was a pity, for she would have been brilliant in the role.

In my New York workshop, two actors brought in a scene from Christopher Hampton's fascinating TOTAL ECLIPSE, about the stormy, bizarre love relationship between the two famous French poets, Baudelaire and Rimbaud. The actors, usually highly capable and interesting, this time wore berets and spoke in the most inexecrable French accents ever heard outside burlesque. I pointed out to them that since everyone in the script spoke the same language, why would they choose to have an accent? You wouldn't do Chekhov with a castful of Russian accents, would you? They were consumed by the accents, scarcely able to make sense of the scene or create a believable relationship.

Many auditors prefer to have you do the scene without an accent at the first reading; then if they find you likely for the role, they will ask you back to do it with an accent. Others want to hear the accent straight off. The best policy is to ask what is wanted.

An Actor Must Interfere with His Partner

A request is not a strong enough motivation for an actor. He must make his needs so strong that he is willing to *interfere* with the other person in order to get what he needs.

Try to make all your goals in terms of interfering. Interference is a demand that you be heard. Most people are so self-absorbed they won't hear you unless you insist.

Interfering means getting in their way so that what you want is stronger than what they want.

The Success of a Scene Is Predicated on the Amount of Need

Your needs must be strong enough so that you will insist that the other person deal with and take care of your problem.

Remember the opposite: You will take care of their problem.

Take.

And give.

Physicalizing Is a Strong Way to Express Feeling

Consider that the actor is onstage a brief time when he does a reading: two to four pages, five minutes, rarely longer. In that brief span he has to let the auditors know everything he can about himself.

One of the most vivid ways to let auditors know about you is through physical expression of what you are feeling. The Chinese say, "A picture is worth a thousand words." A physical image is a strong picture. It sends what you are feeling to your partner and makes an inevitable impact on the auditors.

Consider Marlon Brando's acclaimed Stanley Kowalski in A STREETCAR NAMED DESIRE, one of the most memorable performances because it was so highly physicalized.

Physical expression is not a substitute for feeling but an extension of it. A slap and a kiss are both strong physical expressions of feeling, a touch is stronger than mere yearning, a desire to touch is stronger than abstract interior wishing.

Put your goals in terms of physical images.

Conceive of your actions in physical terms.

Mere inside feeling isn't enough. It has to be *sent* to the partner. Physical interference with your partner is one of the strongest ways to let her know the extent of your demands.

Rhythm

An actor must always use his own natural rhythm in every audition scene. Each of us has his own individual rhythm to which he moves and breathes and talks. When that is interfered with, something unnatural is set up that strikes the auditor as phony, stilted, peculiar, unreal. We sense that something is amiss. You cut off your own life flow if you cut off your own rhythm.

To destroy one's own rhythm is to do a great act of self-immolation. When you deliberately interfere with the life music to which you talk and breathe, you interfere with the truth of your inner feelings. You become unreal to anyone watching you because you are being unreal to yourself.

When I watch soap opera actors struggling to make real that funereal and unnatural pace that is the style of the soap world, I suffer for them because it is a losing battle. When your own rhythm is gone, so is your own life.

Being Square Will Never Win

Most actors tend to make square choices rather than colorful ones because they think square is more real. Square is more usual, and it sure is more dull. In the competition between square versus colorful, colorful wins every time.

No wonder the Salvation Army is so imbued with the air of failure. The outfits that bunch of losers wear make them so unappealing one would rather lie down in the Bowery with a pint than have one's soul saved. If having your soul saved means you turn out to be as square as a Salvation Army lassie with your hair pulled back in a bun and your granny glasses pinching your nose, than the side of the sinners wins.

Ever notice how often the Academy Awards are given to those who portray sinners, while most saints come in as also-rans?

The Negatives Are Always Written

It is a curious wonderment of playwriting to find that the negatives are always written in a play and it is the actor's job to provide the positives.

This means that the no is strongly and literally written:

No, I don't want that
I want to leave
Leave me alone
I won't do what you want

The actor's job is to see through the negative to the other side of the coin, to find the yes that is always also in the scene:

What do you want?
Why are you still there, if you say you want to leave?
If you want to be left alone, why are you still having this relationship?
What do you want to do?

Since many scenes are written about wanting not to be there, it is the actor's job to ask the question: Why am I here?

The positive answer to that question is what motivates the scene.

Actors must learn to remember an important thing: you always have a choice. If you really want to leave, then why are you still there having this scene with this other person? Answer that question and you'll be able to do the scene. Settle for "I don't want to be here" and auditors will have to find for the role another actor who does.

Learn to Use All Levels of Awareness

Actors feel they are really in a scene when they are totally unaware of the audience or of anything except what's going on between them and their stage partners. Therefore they judge themselves harshly—and inaccurately—since this isn't true in life. We can be hearing the radio, we can be watching out the window at someone else, we can be doing the dishes or cleaning the house, and we can be doing four other activities that demand our attention and yet still focus on the partner in a life relationship. Focus means centering attention on the person at hand, not screening out awareness of everything else.

We operate on many levels at once. We're aware of distractions, and we handle them: through focus. You're asking for an unreal situation to be so caught up in your partner onstage that you're unaware of anything else. *Use* the reality of distractions to create focus. That's how we solve the problem in life.

Being Appropriate Is for Performing, Not Auditioning

You don't have to fit the action to the words in the audition situation the way you do in performing. Like an improvisation, impulses may occur that conflict with the words at hand. Go ahead, do the action, trust your impulse. Don't wait for the right moment. He who waits never gets there. Do it now, when you feel it.

Besides, the conflict between the words and your "inappropriate" action can be interesting.

A Long Speech Is Just Several Short Speeches

Actors panic at the sight of a long speech. But you can easily handle it by pretending it is several short speeches, with you creating the rest points en route by seeking response from your partner. Insist on a response before you'll go on. (It need not be verbal, of course.) It will renew relationship and make contact real; and you will avoid just the speaking of written words (which is what long speeches frequently become in an audition).

Overlapping Is Real

Two of the most enchanting actors I ever saw on the stage were Alfred Lunt and Lynn Fontanne. One characteristic of their work was overlapping: one speaking on top of the other one's lines. People do this constantly in life, yet most actors wait patiently for their turn to speak. If actor A should by mistake speak on actor B's line, actor B will stop at once instead of plunging on to get it said, as we in life do.

Of course the Lunts were masters of overlapping, and it is a risk to take in an audition situation. I think it's a risk worth taking, for it is *real*. It provides urgency, it makes actors have to listen to one another, and the life-and-death importance will be encouraged.

Actors Should Be Good Liars

You can usually tell with most actors when the script says the character is lying. They lie so badly, anyone could know.

If your character is lying, lie well. Make it convincing. Most of us lie quite efficiently in life and manage to convince others that we are telling the truth. Why should a stage lie be patently obvious? It takes all the fun out of it.

Scenes Between Actors of the Same Sex Are Always Competitive

That sounds like a bold generalization, doesn't it? True, though. I would say all scenes are competitive, since drama is about what you want versus what I want. Since actors tend to skirt being competitive if it's a scene between members of the same sex, keep in mind that then the competitiveness is even more essential.

Choosing a Need for Comfort Is Never a Good Goal

When you hear yourself using pallid verbs to describe what you are fighting for, know that you are going to give a pallid reading. "Comfort goals" don't work: "I want to be understood," "I want sympathy," "I want to be liked," "I want to be comforted"—all these and similar choices aren't strong enough for readings.

Instead pick a cry for help. Make it desperate, a matter of life and death. Threaten murder or suicide if you don't get help and get it *now*.

It may sound melodramatic, but it works. Weaker comfort choices don't.

"I Don't Care"

Choosing "I don't care" as your emotional attitude toward your partner doesn't work, either. If you don't care, why the hell are we watching the scene? If you don't care, neither do we.

If you don't care, we'll find another actor who does.

Learn to Interrupt Yourself When Ellipsis Occurs in the Script

When the writer has given you an incomplete sentence to say that is supposed to be interrupted by the other character in the scene, you cannot rely in the audition situation on the other actor (or the stage manager) to interrupt you. Too often, the other actor will forget, worried as he will be about his own problems and what he is going to do next, and you can stand there looking very much the wrongdoer while you wait for the move he is supposed to make but doesn't. Make it an audition habit to interrupt yourself by adding to the incomplete sentence one of these thoughts (which you will make active by using it as silent dialogue):

Maybe I shouldn't say this? It might offend him.

Perhaps what I was going to say isn't accurate, so maybe I shouldn't say it after all.

I'd better be careful what I say, or I'll get into trouble.

What was I just saying? My mind wandered.

I'm not going to complete that sentence because I want to see if you were listening.

Similarly, you must be prepared in an audition to receive a bit of business that hasn't been given to you by the other actor. Think: What is more important, your reaction to the event or the creation of the event by your partner? It's your reading, so your reaction is of course more important. So if your partner fails to slap you or kiss you, pretend he has, react to that event as if it did happen. I've seen scenes fall to pieces because an important bit of business wasn't done by the partner, but that failure need not happen to you if you will only create your own event, which is your emotional reaction to the action. You don't need a pistol trained on you in order to be shot, you simply have to fall down and clutch your side.

You can learn to take care of yourself in auditions so that you are not disadvantageously dependent on your partner.

Use "I Don't Believe This" As You Would in Life

In life we frequently have difficulty believing what is actually happening to us. We say, "I can't believe this is happening to me," when it is. When we tell a story that seems incredible, we express our incredulity: "Isn't this unbelievable?" Actors tend to leave this kind of reaction of unbelievability out of their acting. When you find yourself onstage doing something unbelievable, use that fact. It will make what you find unbelievable into something that is believable.

Don't Worry About Indicating Listening

Actors are so concerned with listening that they tend to indicate they are listening. You don't need to show the auditors you are listening. Better by far that you rely on creating specific silent dialogue so that you are reacting to what is heard rather than doing that phony-actor bit of indication. Listening is not external, it is internal.

Should You Be an Actor?

Often actors ask me if I think they should go on trying to be an actor.

I have the same answer for everyone who asks: If you have a choice and could reasonably be happy doing something else, by all means go at once and do something else.

Acting or writing or directing in theatre or television or screen is only for the irrecoverably diseased, those who are so smitten with the need that there is no choice.

5

Monologues, Soliloquies, Style

Actors are frequently asked in an audition situation to bring in prepared monologues instead of a reading. This is most frequently done for auditions for regional or repertory theatre, where many plays are going to be performed and the actor is being considered to become part of a company. Actors are expected to have in their ready-to-perform repertoire at least two monologues: one classical, one modern, one of them to be drama, and the other comedy. An actor would thus do well to have three or four of these ready to perform.

I don't know anything that throws actors into greater panic than having to perform monologues. "What will I do?" they ask, as if there were very little material available to them. Do something you like. I can't quite believe the number of actors who pick material they hate. If monologues are so trying to perform, why pick something that sets you off wrong? Pick something you enjoy, that you're comfortable with, that might even be a pleasure to perform.

Don't be so literal in looking for material. You can arrange a monologue from a play you like by simply removing the spoken words of your partner so you do all the talking. The partner's words that would be spoken in the play can be used by you as silent dialogue responses that will help you create relationship. Make them fast responses, though, not the literal length of time it would take to say the words.

Actors judge the success of their monologue by "how real" they are able to make their invisible partner. Most frequently asked question at the end of a monologue is: "Did you believe I was really talking to someone" or "Did you see my partner?" Waste of time. Auditors aren't interested in your ability to create people who aren't there; the people will be there when you do the play. This is, once again, a classroom dilemma that is blown up into unnecessary importance. To hell with whether you can see someone who's not there; what's important is what *you* are doing.

What you are doing depends on the relationship you create. Relationship isn't dependent on "seeing" someone else, but on *need* for their response. Create response needs from your imaginary partner and forget about trying to "see" them. Nothing is more disconcerting than watching an actor stare constantly into space, working feverishly—and unbelievably—to create someone when there's no one there, which is why this is one time I give you a rule. An absolute rule, from which you mustn't deviate. I call it the *ninety-to-ten rule*. Which is: in a monologue, look at your imaginary partner only 10 percent of the time; 90 percent of your time should be spent seeing images of what you're talking about. Just watch in life whenever someone is doing a long monologue. The person talking is looking at images, only checking back about 10 percent of the time for responses from his partner, in order to be sure she's still following him, to make sure she digs what he's trying to communicate. The one who is not doing the talking does the 90 percent watching, in most cases.

Need is the greatest help in doing a monologue. Needing a specific reaction or series of reactions from your invisible partner. Pick someone you know from your own life to be the invisible partner; don't make up a person. Don't use a literary character for a partner. Use someone you know well. Have a great need for them to give you something specific. Have a great need to change their point of view.

All the usual guideposts apply to monologue work. They must be even more *specific* because there is going to be no one there but you. You need emotional responses from your partner, not merely visual ones.

When there is more than one character in the scene, as is so frequently the case with Shakespeare (where there can be a whole courtful of people for you to deal with), then place the different characters in widely different locations on stage, give them each a single simple attitude toward you that you are either combating or using as agreement.

Staging a Monologue

This is one time you can freely upstage your partner. Put your imaginary partner *downstage* of you with his back to the auditors and his face toward you, then you can use the whole upstage area all for your very own.

Use it.

Actors tend to stand stock still, rooted to one spot, when they do a monologue. The whole stage is yours. Movement can be valuable.

Soliloquy

A soliloquy is talking to yourself when you are alone onstage. It reveals the actor's thoughts and feelings to the audience but not to the other characters in the play, since they aren't there or don't know what you're saying.

What is talking to oneself? It really is talking to other people. When we are dressing to go out, we say aloud, "Now where did I put my keys?" We're not asking ourselves where we put our keys, we're asking someone else. We want someone else to find our keys and tell us where the keys are. In this case, who is the "someone else"? It may be a specific person, such as roommate or wife or husband not present at the time; or it may be that unspecified, mysterious person we all have in our lives to talk to: That Person Who Should Have the Answers.

In another era people talked to God, lifted up their heads and talked directly at Him up there in heaven, just as we've seen Zero Mostel do as Tevya in FIDDLER ON THE ROOF. In this era, where almost everyone is an atheist or an agnostic, we've given up talking to God (although occasionally in moments of greatest stress, we may still say, "God, help me!" and make bargains with Him if He will). Instead we talk to someone who seems to reside here on earth within easy calling distance instead of up in heaven above. While having a conversation with a real-live person, we may look to the left or right, address an imaginary person, and say, "What am I going to do with her?" or "Would you listen to what she just said?" Who is that person we talk to that way? It is someone always sympathetic to our point of view, who will agree with us, rather than the real person we're with. And if you take careful note, you will find most of the time we are asking that imaginary person a question to which we clearly expect an affirmative reply. It's our imaginary lifelong companion, That Person Who Should Have the Answers.

You will often need the companionship of That Person in doing monologues.

In life, we also talk to people we know when we talk to ourselves. Sometimes we have a long conversation directly with one person. This is frequently a rehearsal for something we intend to say to them face to face, or it may be an enactment of a frustration that we will never get to say directly to them.

Sometimes we talk to more than one person. That is the delicious thing about life's soliloquies: We can summon up anyone at will, we can dismiss them at will, we can call them back or send them away in a second. We can people our talking-to-ourselves activities with anyone we know or with the rich and famous we've never known. We are totally in command, which is why talking to ourselves is such a satisfactory experience—and so essential to our well-being.

The process of talking to oneself in life is such a subconscious process that most people don't know they are usually talking to someone else. It's called talking to *oneself*—but in truth we're usually talking to someone whom we imagine to be there with us. It's once again your job, as an actor, to find out in a soliloquy *who* the person is or who the people are to whom you are talking. Once you establish that relationship, doing a soliloquy can become real to you. It's the relationship to other people, real people from his own life, that the actor usually leaves out of his preparation, which is why he has such difficulty doing monologues and soliloquies. Once again, as in any audition work, creating a relationship is the basic essential that the actor must establish.

Soliloquies are regarded with great suspicion by most actors as a mean and alarming stage device invented by playwrights, chiefly Shakespeare, to torture the actor. Nonsense. Soliloquies aren't a stage device; they are lifted right from life. We talk to ourselves all the time. If actors would use life as their source rather than stage convention, they'd find the answers to everything that happens in a play.

Go back to life for your answers. You rely too much on what you've seen other actors do on the stage or screen or television. You forget that every action in a play has a source in life, every so-called stylistic device has its source in life. If you will remember that, constantly, in your work as an actor, your own fantasy/dream life can be the source that will yield the most material.

The aside is another stage device that throws actors. It is easily explained if you think about how we do asides in life, as just discussed. It's simply talking to That Person Who Should Have the Answers, that person with whom we want to share this particular experience. Extend That Person to include the entire audience, and you have a relationship you can work with in doing asides. What is even more fortunate in the case of the aside is that you *can* get response from That Person when it is the audience. How gratifying that can be!

Another important consideration for both monologues and soliloquies: Always have a curtain. Just as the end of a play has a curtain, so should a monologue, preferably a moment for you to hold after you have just delivered a topper to your partner-opponent and you're watching it land and thinking, "Try to top that one, kid." Hold it for the same count you would when you're onstage waiting for the curtain to come down. Too many monologues end with the actor looking frantic and apologetic, as if he were saying, "I know that was awful. Please forgive me. I wish I were dead." Find a moment for the curtain where you are the winner.

All monologues are too long and too slow.

You'll get an A on your report card from the auditors if yours is one of the fast, short ones.

Quality, not quantity.

What Is "Style"?

Actors get so misled by concepts of style.

"Style" is a concept that should be wiped out of an actor's vocabulary. It is a trap, since it usually means to paste something on from the outside. If an actor thinks a play requires "style," he suddenly gives up working subjectively and starts to think objectively—which is always ruin and downfall. He becomes artificial and mannered—and thus unbelievable and empty. God save us all from watching most actors at work doing "style."

Think of style as behavior. Behavior chosen *by the characters* as a way of dealing with the dilemmas of their particular lives. For example, in that scintillating "style" play, THE IMPORTANCE OF BEING ERNEST, the characters are ruled by considerations of real estate. Your address is everything: do you live on the right side of the park or the wrong side, in the city or the country? Real estate is more important than money, because your choice of where you live indicates taste as well as income. Second to real estate is the characters' determination to prove their independence through the expression of opposites. They are perverse. They fight the conventions by decreeing that the opposite of what most people prize is what is more valuable. "You don't know my father? I am happy to say no one does. He never goes out of the house. The proof of manhood is in his being domesticated."

It is important for the actor to realize the characters have chosen to behave as they do. They have chosen, not the playwright or the director. It is their life-style. The playwright is simply the recorder of choices made by the characters. If you ask about a play like THE IMPORTANCE OF BEING ERNEST: what are they fighting for and what games do they choose to achieve this? then you can come up with real, motivated behavior instead of slapping on fake archness. Then you can have real feeling at work underneath the game and role play-ing, instead of being a hollow, empty puppet.

We still play the same games they play in Oscar Wilde or Mo-lière or Sheridan. Real estate is still important to us. Consider how impressed we are if someone has an apartment on Sutton Place South, a house in East Hampton, a villa on the Riviera. Consider the way we compete at cocktail parties to prove who is the wittiest, who is the most sophisticated, who the most in-the-know. Is that behavior so different from Cecily and Gwendolen having tea in the garden?

Ask of a "style" play: what causes the people to choose to be-have this way? Find an equivalent in modern life; it is always there. Motivate your behavior just as you would your own contemporary behavior. The game playing will answer questions of "style." So will the costume. Different clothes cause us to behave in different ways.

Style can become simple. It is a character's choice of behavior, not a playwright's or a period's choice.

One further choice to add: Enjoy how you say what you say. Language is important to the life-style of the characters; they com-pete in the imaginativeness of their use of language. Communication is superior when it is couched in superior language. Enjoy the turn of phrase, *le mot juste*, the flight of fancy, the poetic image. Televi-sion has almost taken enjoyment of language out of our world and given us a steady diet of grubby naturalism, grunted and inarticulate, but there are still modern playwrights who present us with charac-ters who enjoy the way a thing is said: Samuel Becket, T. S. Eliot, Edward Albee, Joe Orton, David Storey, Simon Gray, Ntozake Shange, Enid Bagnold, David Mamet.

6

Pace

Almost every reading I see is too slow.
I have never seen a reading that was too fast.

7

Romance

One great missing ingredient in current acting is romance. Everyone secretly wants romance, but in these harsh, "realistic" days, no one will openly admit it. Romance means you're soft nowadays. We must be hard, to live in the post-Vietnam, post-Watergate era of disillusionment.

But what has made EQUUS such a phenomenal success? Romance. And ANNIE HALL and COUSIN COUSINE and SAME TIME NEXT YEAR and A CHORUS LINE and STAR WARS and PIPPIN. Shakespeare's plays retain their undiminshed popularity because they are everlasting romances. Yet most of the creators of these shows would deny that they are romances. What is worse, most actors, while willing to consider the love and the sex in a scene, are largely unwilling to consider romance when they make their acting or audition choices. Romance has gone out the window. It is time to bring it back.

The Oxford Dictionary uses such words as *imaginative, remote from experience, visionary, fantastic, unpractical, quixotic,* and *dreamy*, to describe romance. It says a romantic prefers grandeur or picturesqueness or passion or irregular beauty to classical finish and proportion. No matter how "classical" our bent, a dream of romance is what no human being can live without; an excess of reality is what is wrong with our current world. Reality kills. We can't live for reality (if we did, most of us could not bear to stay alive for very long) but for the dream of what we hope will happen: love from someone splendid, success, glory, honor, and applause. Romance is the dream of something better happening to us.

People are motivated by dreams, by visions of what might be, not by realities and harsh views of what is. We do not live for what is sensible, yet I am amazed to find actors constantly making rational and sensible choices when they pick their scene motivations.

Of course, we make sensible choices in life, such as going to pick up the laundry in order to have a clean shirt to wear, but drama is not made up of such choices. Plays and films are woven around the unusual choices human beings make, so romance is likely to be the *raison d'être*.

Two actresses were doing that marvelous scene from THE HEIR-
ESS where the aunt comes down the stairs to find that her plain
niece, Catherine, is planning to elope that night with the handsome
and worldly Morris Townsend. The aunt is terribly excited by the
prospect and asks if she can go along on the elopement because
Catherine will "need a chaperone." This actress made only sensible
choices for the aunt: that Catherine would shock everyone if she
didn't have a chaperone (she failed to create the romantic joy of
wanting to *share* in the glorious and audacious elopement); that
Catherine would offend Morris by revealing to him the extent of her
dowry (she did it like a banker, not a woman whose romantic vision
has just been destroyed by the reality of money); that her father
would disown her (sensibly, of course this would be an enormous
loss; romantically, the thought of the revenge against that ice-cold
martinet would be delicious). Without romance, the scene lacked the
gaiety to offset the monetary considerations, the dream to offset the
fear of being left alone. If the scene is only pragmatic and sensible,
it becomes cold, bloodless, charmless. The romance is written into
the scene and yet so many times I have seen actresses do all they
can to avoid it.

For the basis of the scene is the struggle between romance and
reality; both elements exist in both women, in different ways, at different points in life, and at differing maturity and awareness levels.
Unless there are romantic fantasies to feed this scene, it is very difficult to do. The Catherine in this audition was also only sensible in
her view of it: "In order to escape my father, I am going to marry
this nice sensible man, who is going to take me away from all this."
But none of the fervor of excitement at having chosen an elopement.
You would have thought she had arranged through her lawyer for a
trip to city hall for a marriage of convenience.

What feeds a scene like this? Fantasies, dreams, romantic visions. And yet so often the actresses doing it will leave out romance,
flattening what is exciting, making mundane what should be exhilar-
ating and crazy. Perhaps it is the age of psychoanalysis that has
robbed the world of romance. Actors plunge into sensible estimates
of their characters, leaving out the major element of romance, which
will make us laugh, cry, and feel with them.

Bring back romance. It is the secret life that is a primary moti-
vating force in every human being.

8

Musical Theatre

There are few differences between reading for a play and reading for a musical. A good actor can do both (provided he can also sing and dance!). Reading for a musical, however, can pose some special problems:

1. The scenes are concise, tightly and economically written, more like a charcoal sketch than an oil painting. It is the actor's task to provide a rich subtext because today's musicals require a complexity of acting to enlarge and deepen their scope.

2. The climax of a scene is frequently not there in the writing but occurs in the song. In a well-constructed musical, such as A LITTLE NIGHT MUSIC, the song is an extension of the scene and contains its greatest emotional life. Actors unacquainted with working in musicals are sometimes baffled and thrown by this; they feel cheated by the writing instead of learning to extend the emotional line from the end of the written scene through the lyric and the melody.

3. Many times musical scenes are written more for personality than for acting. That is, the scene is constructed on the colorful personality of the star who will play the role rather than on nuances of writing for character. Actors who are not "personalities," then, have a difficult time making anything of the scene, since all the color in the scene isn't written but must be brought to life by the personal qualities of the actor. This is one reason why subsequent companies sometimes cannot achieve the success of the original company. Without an Ethel Merman, CALL ME MADAM is pretty flabby stuff.

4. Musical theatre is fast. But just because the pace is usually faster than a straight play doesn't mean the actor can skate over the surface. Too many musical productions are done that way and are only rescued by the music; the book sections are endured by the audience while they wait for the singing and dancing. The musical actor has got to shoot roots down like a plant, deep. Then go with the rhythm of the wind.

5. Musical theatre is piecemeal; the book is broken up into short scenes. There's usually a major plot and a subplot, a major set of characters and a subsidiary set. While the major set is off changing

costumes and getting a second breath, the subsidiary is onstage doing their stuff. Continuity is hard to find; your scene is over before you know it, the character line you've been working on is snapped, and you have to carry it through to the next scene, which may be two songs and a dance number away. When you're there, you've got to score. Scoring takes roots, deep.

6. Opposites are of vital importance to the actor of musicals. Scenes are frequently written to mean the opposite of what the character says. Since they are brief, the actor must quickly establish important emotional relationships and *needs* from the other character, or it will be two actors doing their stuff straight out and nothing happening between you. This is the grave danger of musical acting.

7. The relationship of the actor to the audience is more direct in musicals. Each twosome scene in effect becomes a threesome, with the audience the third member of the scene. At first this seems artificial until an actor realizes that human beings often create this kind of relationship in life.

When we are having a difficult time making our point to someone in a life situation, we will frequently turn away from our partner to address aloud an imaginary person with words like: "What am I going to do with her? You see how impossible she is!" This is direct address to an imaginary person, a life device frequently gainfully employed onstage.

There is another awareness of audience in life situations. When we are in group situations (three or more people, not necessarily a large group), we will "play to the audience" as a way of amplifying or extending the one-to-one relationship we are having. In such situations we frequently play for laughs. We tend to woo the others in the group to our side, against the side of the other person. "See, aren't I right?" means "See, isn't she wrong?" and if we get support in our viewpoint, it seems stronger and more right to us.

Since there are so many ways of using the audience, indeed downright playing to the audience, in life, a musical actor can always find life justifications and motivations if he will only *observe life instead of the stage*. So many actors I find are constantly using the stage or film as their frame of reference; I always use life. I find everything that happens onstage happens better and more truthfully in life. Since actors have constant trouble finding motivations for the actions the playwright or director has given them, I contend they would find out more truthful and dramatic realities if they would use life as their source. Observe the behavior of human beings! There's where the answers are.

8. Since musical theatre is very fast moving, the actors must find

the *events* in every scene. Even if the strongest events occur in the song that climaxes the scene, there must be events within the scene: Changes in character awareness must be found by the actor and accomplished in such a strong, full manner that the audience will know. Eventless scenes in musicals do not work.

An event in a scene can be subterranean or highly apparent. In a musical it is the actor's task to make sure they occur in the latter manner. This does not mean obvious as opposed to subtle, it means clear as opposed to murky. It means pointed and definite rather than skirted around.

9. Musical theatre is *not* more superficial than drama, a common misconception among actors and audience. I've worked a great deal in musical theatre, and if that skating-across-the-surface point of view were once true, it is no more. Musical theatre is not cutesy-poo and boy-meets-girl and stand-facing-front-and-belt-it-out-to-the-back-row. You do have to play in bigger theatres, so you do have to project more strongly. In many ways musical theatre is more difficult than drama because it needs everything an actor gives to drama and yet it needs *more*. More force, more economy, more relationship (since relationship is split between your partner and the audience, it is even more tricky to accomplish, more complex to handle, more difficult to make real), more humor, more of everything an actor has to offer. To say nothing of singing and dancing as well!

We are talking about acting in musical theatre versus acting in dramatic theatre, although basically there is little difference; the actor should work in the same probing and dimensional way. But what he must accomplish must be done in far less time, so it has to be succinct and immediately total. There is little time for builds and explorations; the actor has to be there with the feeling from the top, or the scene is over with and gone by.

Singing the Song

The most important element in singing at auditions is not the forming of sound but the creation of a relationship. Just as it is in the readings.

Most singers don't, which is why they are dull and lifeless, concerned as they are with making notes and pear-shaped vowel sounds. Audiences are concerned far less with the quality of voices than with the emotional life that is being created. The great singers of popular music are not those with the greatest voices but those who know how to communicate feeling: Peggy Lee, Billie Holiday, Frank Sinatra.

Most audition singing is out front, into the theatre, toward the audience. Since most of us are inexperienced with relating to groups, the singing actor needs to make a relationship that is highly personal and real to him. In his imagination he needs to place out there in the audience a person in the balcony and another person in the orchestra section. He needs to create relationships of strong need to these two people, so that his singing is asking for their response. He should pick highly sympathetic people (like his sweetheart or his music teacher), who are on his side, rooting for him, anxious to approve, and offering emotional response when he sings well to them.

Place these life people in the theatre and sing to them. Not to the auditors, not to an audience, but to real people who mean something to you. Occasionally, you may indeed include the real auditors who are actually there: include them when you feel you're doing well, so that they get you at your most secure. However, do not sing the whole song directly to the auditors (unless they specifically ask you to). I've been listening to actors sing for many years, and I know there is nothing more wearing on the auditor than being sung to! It means I have to be the other half of your love duet if you do that to me; I have to smile encouragingly and send back feelings, when what I want as an auditor is to watch you objectively and judge you, not be the other half of your intensely personal relationship. Include me only occasionally. Your chief drive should be to create a relationship with your chosen partner that is warm, loving, needful.

That's it.

9

Comedy

It's not a democratic thing to say, but I think we must face the fact that one must have an instinct to perform comedy. It can't be learned.

However, the instinct can be so buried under our naturalistic, sledgehammer world that the actor doesn't know he can do comedy. There is little encouragement in most acting classes, evidently, and even less in the world of performing, in spite of the great popularity of the plays of Neil Simon. These few words are therefore offered to encourage the instinct that may be buried deep within you.

The performing of comedy is not basically different from the performing of drama, but there is a different emphasis. Most comedy acting is so dreadful because the actors are trying to be funny. What is worse, they try very hard; every effort shows with laborious groans and creaks, sweat, and buckets of jacked-up and unreal energy lavished on the comedy role. In comedy the *needs* in the relationship must be even greater than they are in drama, the competition is keener and more immediate, the game playing is for life-and-death stakes every move of the way, and one-upmanship is a primary goal of every player.

The major other drawback to most comedy acting is the failure of the actors to use life as their source, which is why their performing is so artificial. All the techniques used in effective comedic acting are also used by people in life; there are, after all, great comedians who never get on the stage or screen and yet perform effectively every day of their lives. Look to life for your source in considering these elements of performing comedy:

Opposites are at the heart of comedy. What makes us laugh is the playing of one emotion *immediately and unexpectedly* against another. Example: "I'm in love, I've never been so happy!" followed immediately by "I wish I were dead" with a total change in emotion. Transitions are the death of comedy. The unexpectedness of the use of opposites, not the telegraphing of them, is the lifeblood of the adept comedy player—in life as well as on the stage.

Competition is essential to comedy. If you don't compete, you lose. Comedy is about the desire to win. It is impossible to be *too* competitive in comedy (if you also have opposites, of course). The game should be played to win, always; the stakes have to be life and death. One of the things that amuses us about comedy is to watch a character making life-and-death importance out of something that we normally do not find important.

Specificity goes hand in glove with competition: you must be highly specific about what you are competing about. Generalities won't create comedy. Actors tend toward generalities a lot when they do comedy, and it isn't amusing. The specifics are frequently picayune, such as wanting a two-minute-and-forty-six-second egg rather than a three-minute egg. The more you break down each beat into its specifics, the more successful comedy is achieved.

Start from a point of innocence: In comedy, as in telling a story, suspense and humor are achieved through the audience's reliving your experience as it happened to you, from the point where you started out innocent of any expectation to the point where you were victimized. Play the opposites: your innocence versus your present sophistication, your innocence versus the occurrence of evil, your innocence versus a cruel and uncaring world.

Knowingness is the basis for the majority of the comedy in Neil Simon, also known as insult comedy. It's the statement of superiority: I know something you don't know, and I intend to let you know it. I'm smart, and you're a fool. I'm in, and you're out. I'm a king, you're a peasant. I'm knowledgeable, you're naïve. Knowingness is a game all of us play in life at one time or another because of the pleasure of being in the know and of lording it over someone else. Some of us play it as a consistent life-style; when the opposite occurs, when our opponent succeeds in being knowledgeable and winning, we are undone. Revenge results. Expert comediennes like Maggie Smith, Tammy Grimes, Carole Lombard, play knowingness versus innocence to devastating comedic result. An enchanting comedy like Noel Coward's PRIVATE LIVES is built on the knowingness of two people who compete to prove who knows the most.

The setup is a polished method of setting up your victim so that he falls into the trap. Then you pounce on him, declaring it's your win. The setup is fiendish; you play at innocence in order to trap your victim, then you let him have it with both barrels. Good, cruel fun. Comedy is rarely based on kindness, it is based on cutthroat competitiveness. Many actors are so determinedly nice that they can't manage comedy at all.

Events are too rarely found by performers in comedy, yet they are essential to the movement of the play. Scorekeeping helps find the events: the celebration of your wins, the marking of your losses. Events must be magnified. The more you make of them, the greater the comedy.

Laying the bomb is a major way to achieve comedy: You lay the bomb and coolly let the other person pick up the pieces. Comedy fails when you can't be cool after you've put the match to the dynamite. In comedy you can never apologize for the risk you've taken or the injuries you've inflicted. The risks are great; only the biggest gamblers get away with it. You've gotta toss out the put-downs and leave 'em lay where Jesus flung 'em. If you try to ameliorate the blow, you will kill the effect. If you comment on the arrow you've shot, then no one will be looking at the target—who should be decimated by the precision of your shoot. Throw the bomb, go into deadpan, let the victim grapple with the results. I see more comedy killed dead by the inability of the actor to trust his shot; he fusses over it and loses the comedy, just as there's no comedy at all if he laughs at his own jokes. Laying the bomb is a life technique, not just for stage use. All of these comedy techniques are from life.

Focus. You can't create comedy by that actor's habit of constantly looking at your partner. Considerable comic effect is created by where you do look. How can you lay the bomb effectively when you're watching your partner to see the effect? What you want is to shoot, hold your deadpan freeze, and then wait for your partner to drop dead. Then look: Oh, you're dead? Good boy.

The focus is on the event and the image of the moment. See that.

The focus is on the image of your intention. See that.

The focus is on the sharpness of what you are describing. See that.

The focus is on the fantasy of what marvelous thing will happen —for example, your partner drops dead at your feet. See that.

Staring into your partner's eyes kills comedy. Don't see that.

Playing to the audience is one very effective focus. We do that in life a lot. We share our reaction to our impossible onstage partner by talking to or needing the reaction of our *imaginary* constant companion, That Person Who Should Have the Answers. Use playing to the audience as you would in real life, not in the phony way most actors do it on stage. There is a world of difference. One is self-involved, self-conscious, unreal, and unbearable. The other is motivated and has real relationship and specific need in it.

Framing is another effective comedy technique, used in real life. It's just what its name implies: putting an imaginary frame around what you're saying so your partner will not be able to miss its importance. You can frame for your partner, or you can frame for your imaginary partner, That Person Who Should Have the Answers. Framing is a way to insist your partner acknowledge your creation of events. It's a way of winning.

Clarity is the flavor of comedy. You can be muddy in drama, but mud sinks comedy, obliterates it. You must be *precise*. You cannot wallow around the moment, the way so many actors do in television acting. I repeatedly use the image of shooting an arrow with a bow: you must hit the bull's-eye. Comedy requires that kind of precision. Clarity and precision are the exact opposite to the style of acting used on soap operas. Recently I was casting a play that required great wit, which is the most precise and targeted of all comedy. As an experiment we auditioned a great many people who act in soap operas. We saw immensely attractive people—bright, charming, interesting—but none of them could deliver the precision that wit requires.

Uh's are the death of comedy. Cut the *uh*'s. Precision means no embroidery. No *uh*'s, *maybe*'s, *if*'s, *and*'s, *but*'s, sighs, giggles, laughs. Actors love to sputter, thinking that creates comedy. One good sputter and the candle's gone out. Be clean.

Be extravagant. I advocate extremities in the use of opposites in all acting, but comedy requires even more extravagant risks. The more immediate the opposite, the better the comedy; the bigger the risk, the better the chance for true humor. Is there any more adroit a comedienne than Maggie Smith, or one who takes more extravagant risks?

Hold the moment. Shoot your arrow, let it land, then hold the moment until someone takes it over. If no one takes over, then pick it up yourself: express an immediate, total opposite, and the game goes on, with you the winner. There is great release in the employment of comedy (in life, I repeat, in life as well as onstage), release from the tragic burden.

Ping-Pong. To repeat: Comedy is a game of Ping-Pong, drama a game of tennis. The faster and more precise the game of Ping-Pong is played, the more brilliant it is. Which is why the habitual funereal pace of the soap opera and, indeed, many of the dramatic shows on television, kills the actor's ability to play Ping-Pong. There is never a game too fast; there is often a game too slow. Watch two people play Ping-Pong. See what pace really is, *life pace*, and bring that to the stage.

Timing is the one you hear about all the time. Comedy *is* based on timing, it's true. Timing is everything. Timing is your very own. No one else can time the way you can. It's instinctual, it's subjective —how can it be taught? The very same line can be said by four different actors: one gets a laugh, three do not. The line rarely gets the laugh; it's timing that does.

It can be argued that all things can be learned, that no one was born with the instinct for comedy timing. Of course, any instinct has to be developed, encouraged, nurtured to grow, must be perfected through trial and error. If actors would stop studying other actors and instead study the way people "time" in life, there would be more who could do the immaculate, secure timing that comedy requires.

Timing is taking a risk. A big risk. You might fall flat on your face. You take the risk of holding, after you've shot your arrow, holding for that fraction of a second while you wait for a reaction (from the partner, from the imaginary companion, from the real-life out-there audience), but cover up the fact that you're waiting. If your waiting ever shows, you're a dead duck. It's quite a game we play, holding for a reaction. Knowing when to start again, knowing when to pounce, when to crow, when you play dumb, when to play smart. It's not just when we do it, it's *what* we do *when*.

That's timing. Comedy lives or dies by it.

Try it. Try it in life. Try it a lot in life. You may get expert enough to carry it on to the stage. Fame and fortune await you if you become truly expert.

I would pay to see you, any night of the week.

10

Simplicity

The actor's process is the distillation of complexities. The simplest choices are the most telling.

When you put it all together, find simplicity.

11

Observations from a Life in the Theatre

What I Look For in an Actor

In my capacity as casting director, I am frequently asked what is the outstanding trait I look for in an actor. My answer is humor.

I doubt there has ever been an outstanding actor who was humorless. Humor is the most private, most distinctive, most personal of all human traits. It is what makes each of us distinct.

If an actor has true humor, and a lot of it, I find he also has intelligence and perception, because humor doesn't develop to a very sophisticated stage without those qualities as a foundation. If an actor has true humor, he makes judgments and distinctions that are uniquely his. If an actor has humor, he's likely to have importance, because humor is the way human beings distinguish what is important from what is unimportant.

A heightened sense of humor means a heightened awareness of other people, therefore a greater desire to communicate and ability to do so. The use of humor in relationships is likely to express a greater sense of and an enjoyment of competition. A willingness to compete, a reveling in competition, means that an actor has drive. An actor must have drive, or he'll never make it. The more *driven* he is, the more valuable he's likely to be—*if* this drive is combined with great humor.

Nobody would want to live in a humorless world. Why would anyone want a humorless actor?

Overacting

When I ask actors why they have made such dull, mundane choices and why they won't take risks with extravagances and extremities, they tell me they are afraid of overacting. I don't know where it came from, but almost all American actors are terrified of overacting. Yet almost all I ever see is underacting.

Where did this ridiculous and widespread fear of overacting come from? Parents afraid their children might march to a different drummer and upset the applecart? Teachers always advocating control of emotions so they won't have to deal with them? Men aren't supposed to cry or show any emotion according to the American myth; women are supposed to be silent and not make waves. Where is all this overacting everyone is avoiding? I rarely see it.

My contention is that there is no such thing as overacting, that one can employ any extravagance of feeling or expression, *as long as there is relationship in it*. What we term *overacting* is done by people who are acting by themselves, narcissistically setting up a storm in which no one else exists. Of course, *this* is unreal. Add relationship, the awareness and need of another, to these very same extravagant choices, and they will be real, lifelike.

It is a never-ending puzzle to me, this unanimous fear of overacting. I spend most of my classes exhorting actors to take risks, show emotion, yell, holler, scream, fight, love, express their feelings *physically*. Most of them nurture tiny little inner emotions. "Who the hell's going to pay any attention to those tiny feelings?" I ask. An expression of feeling isn't worth anything unless it *interferes* with what the other person in the scene wants. If the interference is physically expressed, so much the stronger.

More About the Interview

Most actors hate interviews and would rather do a reading. Rightfully so. An interview is based on your ability to sell yourself, but is that an accurate barometer of your ability to act? Long ago I eliminated interviews from my casting process because I feel it's a waste of time: if someone strikes your interest at an interview, you have them in to read as the next step anyway, so why put everyone through the discomfort of interviews? But I fear the interview is here to stay. Television loves to interview. And some good directors insist on the interview process, for it tells them something about the human being behind the actor, and that human being is what the director is going to work with. Yet I've seen too many occasions when an actor doesn't shine in the interview, so I don't trust them much. A reading or a performance is worth much more.

I was working on a very funny play by James Kirkwood called P.S. YOUR CAT IS DEAD and I brought in an unknown actor named Robert De Niro. Although I'd seen him Off Broadway and in BLOODY MAMA playing one of Shelley Winters' many cretin sons, it was his charm and romance in a small role in a dreadful film, THE GANG

THAT COULDN'T SHOOT STRAIGHT, that convinced me he was the one for the lead role of Vito in Mr. Kirkwood's play. Mr. De Niro came to the interview with his arm in a cast, was shy and inhibited, seemed inarticulate, and was generally hidden and unimpressive. At the end of the day the director went over reactions to the day's interviews with the playwright and producer, deciding who was worth having in to read. Their reaction to Mr. De Niro: "Oh, yes, that boy with the sling—didn't see much there, did you?" Fortunately, when I spoke up to say I thought it very important to hear Mr. De Niro read, they readily agreed. (Some directors and producers don't; I wonder, then, why they hired me, but the ways of the theatre are mysterious to behold.) Robert De Niro's reading was charming, funny, brilliant. That's what you'd expect now, isn't it? But at that time he was almost unknown. They wanted him for the role of Vito.

When P.S. YOUR CAT IS DEAD was postponed for a season waiting for the right actor to costar with Mr. De Niro, he got a role in GOD-FATHER II, and the stage lost another fine actor to film stardom. And once again the pity is that 3,000 miles exist between the place where we make films and the place where we produce plays, so that our actors rarely return to the stage once the films get 'em. Unlike London, where films and plays are done in the same location, where an actor can play on the stage at night and shoot a film during the day, and where it is the custom for actors to do both.

Robert De Niro is the kind of actor who'd have damn few jobs if he had to depend on interviews to get them for him. He auditions brilliantly, he performs even more spectacularly, but at interviews he's a flop. He's shy and introspective; he lives through his acting, not through salesmanship at interviews.

Many actors are like that.

However, we must acknowledge that the interview is a highly prevalent evil, so we must learn to contend with it.

The solution is in the actor's point of view. Try to put yourself in the shoes of the interviewer. Maybe you can then make the whole damnable process easier for both sides: the interviewer has to sit there all day long, drawing people out, finding out who they are, discerning talent and bizzaz. The interviewer is confronted, as mentioned earlier, largely by frozen actors who want to recite their résumés in a singsong and reveal themselves not at all. Or we have their opposites: the actress so busy being Sparkle Plenty that you get the feeling you've wandered into a reunion of Howard Johnson hostesses.

If the actor were to put it in his mind that his task is to *help* the poor interviewer, it might be easier for both sides. If the actor were to regard the interviewer as a fellow human being instead of an executioner, if the actor could make it into a social situation where it's possible he could meet someone he might like, someone he can chat with and feel free with, then there would be a chance some communication might take place. Most interviews are totally deficient in any form of communication, becoming empty rote rituals, when communicating is what they're all about. Try to *see* the interviewer, get hip to him, sensitive to what he might want to talk about. Since usually your résumé is right there on the desk, why discuss your résumé? Talk about anything else: an experience you had on the subway, how you got mugged or raped last night, the funny way your dog bit your mother-in-law. Something pleasant, inconsequential, purely social, to break the ice and give you both a chance to relax.

Once I had an interview with Jerome Robbins. I sat along with a group of actors in his waiting room until it was my turn. When I got into his office, he was, of course, on the phone, so it gave me time to study the painting that hung over his desk. I remarked on the painting when he got off the phone and we spent the entire interview enjoyably discussing painting. We had a good time. I left him studying my résumé. I got the job.

Of course it's a risk discussing painting instead of the project at hand, but a remark or two will soon tell you, *if you are sensitive*, if the interviewer wants to talk about painting or if you should make an immediate shift in subject. The interview is an even bigger risk than the reading, so be prepared to take the risk of opening up; isn't that always a better risk than sitting there tight as a clam so that nothing at all is revealed about you? Actors have this mistaken notion that if nothing is revealed, they have kept themselves from making a mistake. The mistake *is* to reveal nothing. No one is going to hire a frozen robot to do a vivid job of acting.

Luck

For a long time I resisted the belief that luck had something to do with what one achieved. I inherited the old Puritan belief that if you worked hard and persisted, you would win. Turns out no such thing.

There are talented people who work hard their whole lives through and never get the recognition they deserve, because the fortunate accident of being in the right place at the right time never did happen for them.

Consider actors like Al Pacino and Robert De Niro and Barbra Streisand and Elliott Gould and George Segal, who well might never have made it in the days of Gary Cooper and James Stewart and Randolph Scott and Errol Flynn and Leslie Howard and Ray Milland

and Fred MacMurray, when a leading man was English, WASP, or wholesome middle America. Now ethnic is in, and these remarkable performers have made it, though in another era they could have been ignored.

But you gotta be ready when luck comes your way, so persistence and discipline and hard work are still essentials to success. Take Robert Redford. I saw him in two or three small roles in insignificant Broadway flops before I had the task of casting the leading man in a Norman Krasna comedy David Merrick was producing called SUNDAY IN NEW YORK, which Garson Kanin was directing, I wanted Mr. Redford to come in to read for it, but he was in California trying to get a break in television or film. His agent told me he was broke and it was hard for him to afford to come to New York to try out for SUNDAY IN NEW YORK. Fair enough, I said. Let me comb the woods here completely and when we get near the finish line, I'll call you and have Mr. Redford come then. It was the final day of casting, and Mr. Redford had thumbed his way from Hollywood to read. He got the part and very good notices, and although the play itself was not a success, Mr. Redford was seen in it by Mike Nichols, who put him in BAREFOOT IN THE PARK, which was a success. Mr. Redford's career has zoomed ever since.

The timing was right. I helped by not having Mr. Redford in to read until we'd seen every other available leading man, so by then the director and the playwright were ready to consider an unknown, even if he was a blond. (Before Robert Redford, it was a customary show biz belief that a blond actor could never make it. The evidence was that none ever had. Gene Raymond was the exception that proved the rule.) But Mr. Redford was ready when that bit of luck came his way, disciplined, hardworking, talented, and persistent.

Perhaps you feel that Robert Redford would have made it one way or another, sooner or later. When a man is as talented and as attractive as he and Paul Newman are, one tends to think they couldn't miss. Not true. The woods are filled with those who missed, frequently because they weren't persistent or disciplined or *driven*, but sometimes because they were never in the right place at the right time.

If you doubt it, it may be more clearly illustrated by the example of painters and writers, many of whom are unacknowledged or even reviled in their lifetimes but achieve fame and glory posthumously. That's not a choice open to an actor, fame after death, because his work medium is not a canvas or a piece of paper but his living and breathing self.

Persistence

I suppose that anyone who makes it in any field must be persistent, but it seems that actors must be even more persistent, since there are about five thousand applicants for every acting job. Most actors fail not because of lack of talent but because

1. They don't work hard enough
2. They aren't disciplined
3. They are literal rather than truly imaginative
4. They are victimized by their limitations and prejudices
5. They are ruled by their negative side
6. They are not persistent

Actors, just like most of us, take no for an answer. An actor cannot afford to.

I am not saying you will get what you want if you persist. I am saying you will get *considered* for what you want if you persist. There are too many subjectives, unfathomables, and imponderables in casting to allow any actor to think that if you keep on trying, you'll get the role you want. Whether or not you get the job cannot be the criterion, but only the security of knowing that you have auditioned well. Remember: you can audition better than anyone for a given role but still not get it because you are too tall or too short, too slim or too wide, too handsome or too ugly, too young or too old, too like the leading man in type. It's even possible you remind the director of his accountant. Casting is a highly subjective process, as are all the creative elements in theatre and film.

One of the reasons I am a great believer in persistence is not only because I have seen that the persistent actor is the winning actor but because of my own personal experience. When I was William Hammerstein's assistant in creating the New York City Light Opera Company, I did the casting as well as the myriad other chores done by a producer's right-hand man, but what I wanted next for myself was to become a casting director on Broadway. The most prolific producer at the time was David Merrick, so I started a letter campaign. Once a week for seven months, I wrote David Merrick a letter in which I suggested he consider me to be his casting director. I never complained to him when I heard nothing from him. Instead, I made the letters chatty and informal, largely about Mr. Merrick's activities —fortunately, they were voluminous, so there was always a lot to chat about—and what I thought of other Broadway productions. I was careful not to make the letters very long. My goal in each was to be pithy. And, I hoped, entertaining.

When the months went by with no interest shown by Mr. Merrick, I began a second campaign in addition to the letters and asked all the people I knew to mention me to him if ever the opportunity arose. It finally did, One night in Hollywood (I love stories that contain the phrase *one night in Hollywood*, don't you? It seems to me the apogee of unreality) the wife of a close friend happened to find herself seated next to Mr. Merrick at dinner, so she launched into a recitation of the virtues and valuable imagination of Michael Shurtleff. I thought that would surely do the trick, but nothing came of that, either. I increased my letter campaign. Now Mr. Merrick got letters twice weekly.

A few weeks later, finally the call came. In the nick of time, as they say, because I suspect I was soon to be out on the street. At the time, I was working stopgap for Ethel Linder Reiner, a colorful and extremely wealthy producer who somehow got me confused with the butler, since, when she came into the office in the morning, she expected me to jump up from my desk and take her mink coat off her shoulders and hang it up in the nearby closet. This task became increasingly irksome to me. The sound of her big, elegant feet coming down the hallway set my teeth on edge: here comes butler time. One day I busied myself at the typewriter, pretending not to notice her arrival, while she stood there waiting to have her mink taken from her shoulders. "I'm waiting," she said. "I know you are," I said and went right on typing. She dropped her mink on the floor and marched into her own office, slamming the door behind her. The mink stayed there the rest of the day. Messengers and visitors stepped on it or around it until one kind soul picked it up and put it on a chair. Then people sat on it. Mrs. Reiner spoke to me in tones of ice. After that fervid expression of masculine independence, it was soon time for me to move on; Mrs. Reiner was not a lady to hang up her own minks. The next day Mr. Merrick's secretary called, saying merely that the great Mr. M. would talk to me on Friday at three.

We talked, to my surprise, for two hours. In all that time Mr. Merrick said nothing about my expressed goal of becoming his casting director, so at five P.M. I said I had enjoyed our talk but I had better be getting back to work. (I had visions of a future of hanging up mink coats.) With my hand on the knob ready to depart, thinking show biz was even more bizarre than I had imagined, Mr. Merrick said, "Well, see you Monday." "Uh," said I, "why will you see me Monday?" "Your letters said you wanted to work for me," said Mr. Merrick, "so start on Monday."

So I believe in letter campaigns. I believe in persistence, in leaving no stone unturned, in refusing to be ignored. Directors and actors frequently say to me, "How can I get a job? I would even act or direct without pay." When I tell them to contact all the Off-Off-Broadway producers, writers, and directors, they say, "I've done that." It turns out they've called or written once, received no answer, and hung up their hat. If you want something, you have to keep after it. Nobody's waiting to hand you anything you want without your effort. Ceaseless, persistent effort.

Bette Midler persisted. When she took my class, I found her extraordinarily talented (I didn't have to teach her about humor) but in a glum state. "This business doesn't want me," said she, "I'm going to get out of it." We all think that, and often. Only the irreparably smitten can persist. I had the feeling Bette Midler didn't mean it; we say we're getting out in order to threaten ourselves into some positive action. When her long run in FIDDLER ON THE ROOF was getting her nowhere, she took the risk of singing at a homosexual Turkish bath on Saturday nights, after her Broadway stint. It led to stardom in her own show at the Palace, her own record albums and TV shows, and now her own films.

Lily Tomlin was another cabaret performer who took my class. No matter what she did, we all laughed. She was a very funny lady. "You see how awful it is," she said. "I want to be taken seriously, and everyone always laughs at me." But she persisted, from cabaret back rooms to supporting roles on TV comedy hours to creating her own characters on "Laugh-in" and then on up the ladder to her one-woman show on Broadway. She found her own delicate balance between her comic talent and her ability as an actress. People take her seriously now. She'll next be writing, producing, and starring in her own films.

Robert De Niro peristed. Many were the lean years, working in the lofts and byways of Off-Off-Broadway, the humiliation of interviews where he knew he seldom impressed, doing quickie independent films or supporting roles. Nothing came easy. It rarely does.

The People Who Make It

The actors who make it work hard. Having watched actors most of my life, working closely with them, listening to them, teaching them, I find this a frequently overlooked reality. Not many Americans work hard, but they expect glory anyhow. Working on THE MATCH-MAKER, I discovered that every single night of the year's run Ruth Gordon came to the theatre an hour before the rest of the cast and onstage alone went over all her stage moves and her part to keep it fresh and disciplined and new. What most actors don't know is that "newness" comes from discipline, not from inspiration. Inspiration is great in rehearsal, but for a long run, only discipline, the heart of

technique, can keep a performance alive. When I worked on JA-
MAICA, I'd find Lena Horne rehearsing with her musicians every
Wednesday and Saturday between matinee and evening performances, perfecting that easy, "natural" style of hers. (It was one of the
pleasures of my life to sneak into the shadows at the back of the
house to watch her work.) A year and a half after the opening of PIP-
PIN, when he'd won a Tony for his performance, one could find Ben
Vereen still rehearsing his role in the afternoon before a performance. You have to be lucky to make it, for there are undoubtedly talented people who don't, but you have to be ready when the break
comes. You can't be ready without hard work. To stay there once
you've made it requires unceasing hard work and discipline. Luck
aside, the reason a lot of talented actors don't make it is because they
don't work hard. I would hazard that in the years of teaching actors,
I've found that 85 percent of them don't. Sadly, most of them don't
know this about themselves. They daydream of being an actor, con-
fusing desire with discipline.

Age Can Be Irrelevant

I also used to sneak into the giant St. James Theatre and sit
in the back to watch Sir Laurence Olivier and Anthony Quinn rehearse BECKET. Since I had cast the show, I was permitted an occasional surreptitious visit. Sir Laurence rehearsed in his braces (we
call them suspenders) and peered at Mr. Quinn and Peter Glenville,
the director, over his spectacles and seemed a very old, uncertain,
soft-spoken creature. He mumbled; I never did hear what he said,
except it seemed to be, "Do I move to the left on that line?" How
in the world were we going to get a Becket out of these rehearsals?
I wondered.

At the first preview, I happened to be backstage when the stage
manager announced places. Sir Laurence's dressing room was immediately off stage left. He came shuffling out to wait in the wings for
his first entrance. Still no signs of young Becket. My heart was sink-
ing. Suddenly, before my very eyes, Sir Laurence drew himself up,
straightened his shoulders, tossed off twenty-five years by a sheer act
of will, and onstage went the youthful Becket, romantic, daring, spir-
ited, humorous, and spellbinding. Isn't it curious how great actors
surmount age?

Why I'm a Strong Advocate of Risk-Taking

The second story about Barbra Streisand has a moral.
After her first theatre audition for me, I wondered what I was go-

ing to do with this strange-looking, very young woman with the marvelous voice. I had her in a couple of times for shows and the reaction was, "She sings great, but what can we do with a girl who looks like that?" I persisted. Along came I CAN GET IT FOR YOU WHOLESALE by Jerome Weidman and Harold Rome, to be directed by Arthur Laurents (a remarkable theatre man with an unusual eye for new talent, as I'd discovered working with him on Ethel Merman's GYPSY and Stephen Sondheim's ANYONE CAN WHISTLE, in which we cast Lee Remick and Angela Lansbury and Harry Guardino). I thought the role of Miss Marmelstein in WHOLESALE might just fit Miss Streisand.

I scheduled her last the day of her audition. She arrived late, rushed on stage in her famous raccoon, explaining she was late because she'd seen the most marvelous shoes in a thrift shop window and just had to go in to get them. Only one of each pair fit, but she loved them anyhow and didn't we think they were wonderful? She was wearing two unmatching shoes, the first time any of us had seen this phenomenon, which I presume Miss Streisand invented, since it later became a fashion. She started to sing and then stopped after two notes, chewing gum all through this rapid-fire monologue, saying she must have a stool, could anyone find a stool for her, please? By this time the auditors were muttering at me, "Where did you find this nut?" and getting ready to kill me with dark looks as they started to slink from the theatre. She sang the first two notes of her song, then stopped again. This time to take the gum from her mouth and squash it on the underside of the stool. Then she sang. She mesmerized 'em.

They asked her to sing two more. After that, they converged on the stage to explore their new discovery up close. They were Arthur Laurents; Herb Ross, the choreographer; Jerome Weidman and Harold Rome, book and score; and the various associates and assistants who come to the auditions of big musicals. David Merrick, who was the producer, took me to the back of the house alone.

"I thought I told you," he said, "that I didn't want ugly girls in my shows!"

"I know, David," I said, "but she's so talented."

"Talented, shmalented, I don't want ugly girls in my shows. We had this out on CARNIVAL. Now you're doing it to me again."

"But—"

"There's no buts! Look at them, swarming all over her. They love her! What am I going to do now? I'll never get rid of her!"

David Merrick stormed off with gleams of resentment firing from both cannons. I was in for it this time. I went onstage to be congratulated by Arthur Laurents for my find, Miss Barbra Streisand. I smiled weakly. Being persecuted by Mr. Merrick was a small price to pay for such a discovery, I thought grimly, preparing for a life of hell, when Mr. Laurents called me back. Miss Streisand and all the others had gone; Mr. Laurents was alone, sitting onstage on the stool Miss Streisand had commandeered.

"Look at this," Arthur Laurents said to me. "Run your hand over the bottom of this stool."

I did. There was no gum. She hadn't recovered her gum; Arthur had been watching to see if she would. There had never been any.

"My God," said Arthur, "what have we got on our hands this time?"

It was the first inkling of what an incredible actress this young singer already was: an adventuress who at eighteen had her shit together so strong, she took the risk of putting on an act about a raccoon coat, shoes that didn't match, a stool, and a piece of imaginary gum.

It wasn't long after that Mr. Merrick was paying her five thousand dollars a week to do FUNNY GIRL. He withdrew his name from the production, I was told for some complicated legal reason, but I think he couldn't own up to being the sponsor of an ugly girl being the biggest star on Broadway.

The moral of the story: Take a risk.

You may fall flat on your face, but they'll at least remember you.

P.S. Earlier, I said, "Never chew gum at an audition."

In another spot I said, "It's the exception that proves the rule."

About Directors

Directors are a strange breed. Stranger, even, than actors. The good ones have a mystique all their own; they are rare and are to be highly treasured. The bad ones are fakes, trying to create mystery and authority out of sheer not knowing. Most directors are bad directors. They know little and are almost totally resistant to learning. They pretend to know everything, which makes them almost impossible to deal with, since only the desire to learn leads one to being open and creative.

Actors spend most of their lives dealing with bad directors. Talk to any good and experienced actor, and he will tell you that he has worked very seldom with a good director. This book is designed to teach an actor how to function even with a bad director. Since most of his life is spent with directors who interfere more than they help, an actor damn well better learn how to function in spite of them. What is saddest and most frequently destructive about bad directors is that they don't know how the actor functions, what his needs are, and how to create an ambiance in which the actor can work. Worse, they don't want to know. They want to direct. Most of them think directing is telling other people what to do.

A good director shares, not tells. He creates an environment that enables the writer and the actor to work. His job is to explore the play with the actors, find out what they know and lead them to know more, sense what they feel and get them to express their feelings. The rehearsal process is the actor's time to experiment, to indulge in trial and error, so the commitment of error is just as important in the process as the discovery of what's right. How is an actor to know what is right for him if he hasn't gone through being wrong? A good director encourages actors to find themselves in the roles, not fulfill some preconceived image. A good director knows that the channels of communication between him and the actor and between him and the playwright must remain clear and open. He works hardest to achieve that.

There are two levels of directors: successful ones and unknown ones. I've worked with both. The successful ones all have one thing in common whether they are good or bad directors: they are curious about human beings. They may be megalomaniacs and they may be Carried Away by Concepts that blind them to the play at hand, but they are curious and interested in what those human beings are doing up on that stage. They may not know how *to communicate* to actors (I'm convinced only a handful of directors know that), but they are curious.

The unknown directors remain unknown, for the most part, because they lack curiosity about the actor as human being. I've spent years working with new directors in New York workshops. Most of them are a sorry lot, imbued with the idea that directing is Telling Other People What to Do. Some come to me and say, "Those actors won't do what I tell them!" Most of them charge through like bulls at a feast of virgins, ravishing everyone in sight, overwhelming them like Zeus, pillaging and destroying, all in the name of Their Concept of the play. Most directors would like best to do a play in which there were no actors, if they could just make Their Concept known.

What is even worse is that most directors have no curiosity about playwriting, about what makes a play tick, how it is put together, how they can help make a play realize itself by working with the writer. They have no curiosity about their own craft and little willingness to learn. They simply want to Do It: Get Those Actors and Insist on Their Concept. Most directors should go into puppet work, so little are they equipped to deal or interested in dealing with human beings.

Since this sad summary is all too true, actors must learn to take care of themselves. They must learn to keep communication open with the director no matter how he tries to ride roughshod and bully them, no matter how little he is interested in them, no matter how little he knows about the play that is being rehearsed (and some of them seem to have read a different play from the one being produced), even when he gives them line readings and tells them to look and talk like Lana Turner. Actors tend to declare war on directors, which sinks the project, of course. Most plays we see are sunken projects, the result of the war between actors and directors. There's no point in warring with the director: nobody wins. The director gets more stubborn about His Concept and gets more oblivious to the needs of the particular actors because he becomes more resentful of them. Since there is no victory possible (indeed, does war ever accomplish any true victories?), actors must learn how to keep communication open. Then discover how to do in your own way what the stubborn man is saying.

It won't be easy. Communication with someone who is deaf, dumb, and blind never is. But keep trying. If you learn to translate his views into actions that you can accomplish in *your* way, the project has a chance. Declare war and all is lost.

Actors usually have much more training and experience than most directors. It makes logical sense, then, that it is the actor who has to keep the production afloat. It is the actor, not the director, who has to get out on the stage and be viewed by the audience. So you damn well better learn to keep communicating! You've got no other choice.

Actors could accomplish communication if they put their minds to it, if they'd stop carping and complaining about the director. We all know most directors are inept, so don't waste time announcing the known news. Get to work listening to the man: is there anything in his highfalutin talk that you can use? Is there a way to coax him into looking at what you'd like to try? Woo the man. You may get a good performance out of such a courtship.

A note of sympathy to directors: if I sound unduly harsh on you, I mean to be. You are for the most part an arrogant lot, unwilling to learn. I can put up with your inexperience and even with your desire to dominate, but your refusal to learn anything is what makes you so irritating. However, I do also know that actors can be as stubborn and intractable as you are, as unable to listen, as unwilling to explore, as filled with prejudice and blind spots, and just as hard to work with and just as closed-minded. I know there are times when they should be strangled or fired and replaced with computers, but they are all we've got.

There's only one solution to this endless misunderstanding between actor and director: communication. If you keep the lines of communication open, really make a total effort to keep receiving what is being sent to you, even the most opposite of views can be made into a rewarding theatre experience.

Unfortunately, as E.E. Cummings pointed out, most people are amorous of misunderstanding.

A Very Brief Story for Directors

I didn't cast all of Richard Burton's HAMLET but was only called in by producer Alexander Cohen for an emergency one-shot job. Normally I turn them down, figuring I'm not a troubleshooter but a casting director who needs to be part of the creative effort from the beginning, not doing patch work after it's all too late; but this was to work with director John Gielgud on finding a new Ophelia. I'd never worked with Sir John so I said an immediate yes. It turned out it was not Sir John's idea to fire the actress he had; the producer and others wanted her replaced, so Sir John pacified them by coming into New York from the pre-Broadway tour for a day of auditioning new Ophelias. British directors, I note, are always reluctant to fire an actor, feeling that, since they chose 'em, it must be at least half their fault; whereas American directors are often eager to give someone the sack.

Sir John was very polite. "These are very nice gurrls," said Sir John, "and I thank you for showing them to me. I'll think about them all, very carefully." But I knew he was going to go right on with the Ophelia he already had, working with her privately night after night, after the performance, in hotel rooms, wherever, because if she wasn't good now, it was his duty to go on with her until she was.

This story has an important moral for directors: Really good directors take responsibility for the performances of their actors.

Most directors don't, which is why they aren't good at their profession.

Who Does the Casting?

Since no one seems very clear about what a casting director does, let me explain, since it might be helpful for actors to know. Casting directors do not cast. Directors, writers, and producers cast. Most often, directors carry the biggest weight in the decisions that are made about casting. Casting directors work closely with the director. That is the key relationship in a casting director's life, since it is the casting director's job *to find* what the director wants in each role.

This means that the casting director does the screening: he interviews actors, he auditions actors, he sees them perform in plays and on screen. He needs to know the actor's work, so he sees a hell of a lot of productions. In my days with David Merrick it was not unusual for me to see ten or twelve productions a week, on Broadway, Off Broadway, Off-Off-Broadway in the various locations where plays are done. I see most films; I even watch television, although I find that medium is the most perplexing and most unrewarding judge of an actor's ability.

If he's clever, when a casting director makes a discovery, he'll set it up carefully so that the director and the producer will feel they've made the discovery of the new talented young actor. When the director or writer or producer doesn't like his suggestions, he must keep well in mind that he isn't directing the show, the director is. And the director is the fellow who's going to have to work with that actor, so it's his instincts that must at all times be respected. I don't mean to imply that the casting director isn't highly influential; he's usually on the project because the director trusts his judgments. And he is the one who decides who the director does see. But remember that the casting director *suggests*; he does not cast. It's his job to know a lot about a lot of actors, so that he can advise and present to the director the best of the existing possibilities.

On Arrogance—And Being Likable

The casting of JESUS CHRIST SUPERSTAR (I did the Broadway stage version and the film as well as the original touring concert companies) was a most bizarre and engaging experience. The producer, Robert Stigwood, is an astute, colorful, sometimes astonishingly perceptive man, as a producer should be; but he's from the world of rock music and is different from any other Broadway producer with whom I've ever worked. I found him ingratiating and very amusing, with a sly, wicked sense of humor and a desire to turn everything into a party. (We had lobster and champagne for the final day of auditions!)

Casting the show was like doing a Cecil B. DeMille spectacle via Barnum and Bailey; I wouldn't have missed it. I auditioned for weeks from early morning to late at night, seeing any kid who stood in line on the street outside the theatre and thought he or she could sing the music. A lot of the actor-singers we used had never been on a stage outside of their community or high school; most have never been heard from since, for while they could sing SUPERSTAR and some had talent, few had the discipline necessary to make it in the theatre world. For them it was a jolly jaunt, and they eased the pain with their bag of drugs.

Tom O'Horgan, the director, is an erudite middle-aged hippie, highly knowledgeable musically, an unfailingly polite and charming man who regards most other middle-aged folk as obsolete. His fascination with and appreciation of the young gave us the beautiful HAIR and the spectacular JESUS CHRIST SUPERSTAR. He had a great eye for the talented kid, but he was blinded by one strong prejudice: If he thought anyone was "plastic," that was the end of 'em. "Plastic" meant having short hair, bathing regularly, not being drug oriented, looking the boy-next-door respectable. He'd have given the gate to Robert Redford fast. The fact that a different kind of nonconventionality might exist under the "plastic" exterior did not interest Tom O'Horgan—perhaps rightly so, for he was doing visual work.

He was polite to me and frequently asked me my view of those who were auditioning. Then he went on his merry way casting his various alumni from the 101 companies of HAIR that had been done all over the country—and the world. For his concept of the show, he was right. It worked, JESUS CHRIST SUPERSTAR was a success, no matter what I thought of it. Perhaps it was his view of me as one of the plastic ones that excluded me from the final powwow on the choice of principals for the show. The director, the producer, the writers, and the musical director went out to the lobby of the Mark Hellinger Theatre after the final auditions, while I was left sitting in the stalls. This surprised me, for I haven't worked on a show in years in which my views were of so little interest to the creators who were, after all, paying for them. I could have been of help to Mr. O'Horgan, for I agreed with his choices.

Fate was on our side that day, in its ironic style. In the end I was able to help Mr. O'Horgan get Ben Vereen for the role of Judas (which was his choice from the beginning; it was he who had flown Ben in from San Francisco to audition for the role). In the battle between the two camps over which actor was to play Judas, it turned out that the musical director had the deciding vote.

The musical director had never done a Broadway show before. He and I got along like a house afire because I was willing to explain the whole process of Broadway casting to him and my thinking on the 2,001 auditions we went through for that show. He was gratifyingly interested in learning what considerations went into casting; we had a good time together. When the voting in the lobby reached a stalemate, the musical director sneaked into the Hellinger auditorium and asked me, "Who should I vote for? Stigwood wants Candidate A, O'Horgan wants Ben Vereen, the writers are splits, and mine is the vote that will decide." I said, "Vote for Ben Vereen." "Why?" asked the musical director. "It's clear," I said, "from the fact that they've reached a stalemate that both actors are very talented, they both sing extraordinarily well, they've both got charisma [a favorite phrase of the time], there is an excitement and an intensity about each of them. But where Candidate A seems remote and disdainful, Ben Vereen is loveable. We should be able to sympathize with Judas in this play. And audiences don't like an actor who is disdainful of them, although they may admire him." I argue this point constantly in the world of casting: You're always ahead if you cast a performer who is likable. Unlikable performers can sometimes have long, even important, careers, if they have talent, fascination, sexuality, and uniqueness, but some odd chemistry always happens in their relationship to an audience. Frequently the audience does not know they don't like a performer, but they are disturbed by him (or her), and the elements work in a strange, frequently unpredictable way. I have seen too many productions in which the actor comes off with great notices and the project fails—because the actor is arrogant.

Why Didn't You Get the Role?

The girl who gave the most exciting auditions (she did three of them) for the role of Mary Magdelene in SUPERSTAR was Bette Midler, already a celebrity at this time. Bette had taken my class in how to audition when she was in FIDDLER ON THE ROOF, playing a small role. She was extraordinary even then, and memorable, but she was disheartened at that time by her long tenure hidden among the supporting players of FIDDLER. She felt she deserved leads. She was right.

Bette Midler sang "I Don't Know How to Love Him" like no one else: disillusioned, hurt, vulnerable, with the pain of a Mary Magdelene who had been made to believe again after she was determined not to because of the hurts she had experienced. Tom O'Horgan adored her and was strongly tempted (even though Stigwood and the writers were always in favor of the woman who had done the record, Yvonne Elliman), but eventually, I think, he realized this mature, voluptuous, womanly interpretation of the role would not fit in with his cast of hippies and flower children. He couldn't quite let her go, though. I was asked to bring her into the theatre to wait for Mr. Stigwood to arrive. "Miss Midler," I said, "if you would be so kind . . ." And without acknowledging our previous association with each other, I led her to her seat. En route she whispered to me, "Don't give me away," and I didn't, for I realized a superlative performance of a celebrity star was being given to surround the audition itself. She was regal and mysterious, this Mary Magdelene, and she revealed not an ounce of the marvelous honky-tonk performer she was to be in her one-woman shows.

I tell this tale to show that actors must not worry about why they don't get a role; they should only concern themselves with doing the best damn audition they know how to do. Midler did brilliant auditions for SUPERSTAR, but she was not cast because it would have disrupted the casting of the rest of the show. Many times I have heard directors say about an actor: "That is the best audition we'll ever see of that role. Too bad we can't cast him." Their regret is genuine. But there has to be a balance in casting—the parts must fit like a jigsaw puzzle—and there are times when the best auditioners don't "fit."

An actor cannot concern himself with that; there lies madness. Just go ahead and audition well, cry a little when you don't get the role you want, but never ask why. The why is usually a series of imponderables over which the actor has no control.

Always Give It a Try

There is a second chapter to the Ben Vereen story.

I doubt that any audience had a clear view of the actors in JESUS CHRIST SUPERSTAR. They were hidden behind masks and weird costuming and they were used as figures in a giant puppet show. Ben Vereen's vivid portrayal of Judas went unnoticed, and the director became the star of the show. Okay.

A year later I was casting PIPPIN for director Bob Fosse and producer Stuart Ostrow. One of the characters was identified as The Old Man, but because he was the ringleader of a band of roving players in the play, we termed him The Leading Player—partly to get away from The Old Man concept, which we found through auditioning wasn't going to bring much life to that inert part. "We need someone vivid for the part," Fosse said to me, "and I'd love to have a dancer." An old man dancer? We went on auditioning, every character man in town. For some reason, most of them hadn't kept up on their dancing.

When I mentioned Ben Vereen, with grave hesitation, I discovered Fosse had used him as a dancer in his film version of SWEET CHARITY. I sent the script of PIPPIN to Ben and asked him to prepare an audition. What he brought in was sensational. He took the scenes from the script for The Old Man, paltry as they then were, and around them he wove three singing numbers, ending up in a big dance solo. For the first time, our "Old Man" came to life in the person of a young, sexy, humorous black actor who was an irresistible singer and dancer. The role was enlarged and rewritten for Ben Vereen. He walked off with the show.

Moral of the story: If they ask you to audition for an eighty-year-old character man and you're a handsome young leading man, go audition anyhow. You just might change their minds completely. They just might rewrite the show around you.

Actors complain that producers and directors lack imagination. So do actors. They're prone to tell me, usually through their equally nonimaginative agents, that they're "not right" for a role for which I've asked them to audition. That's nuts. How do they know? If they're actually asked to come in to audition, they should take the time to do so. Does an actor really know what he's right or wrong for? Since he doesn't know what the concepts are in the minds of the director or the casting director, how can he make this judgment? During the process of casting a new show, concepts change constantly. That's why I like working with Bob Fosse: an eighty-year-old dreary character part is cast with an exciting new black performer who becomes a star, a colorless character woman in CHICAGO is cast with a female impersonator with a phenomenal soprano voice (the actor had never impersonated females before), for the straight leading lady in PIPPIN we cast an expert, light Carole Lombard–style comedienne, for the mother in PIPPIN we cast a sexy young dancer so that Mr. Fosse could turn the role into a funny satire on the classic gold digger, for the sentimental old grandmother we cast the salty vaudevillian Irene Ryan. All were cast against the conventions of the roles as written. Yet there were actors whom I asked to audition who said, "I'm not right for the role." It should be a cardinal rule of an actor's life: *Always audition*. You may find out something about the role you haven't gleaned from the written page; you may find the director has a concept totally unlike the writing. Half an actor's life is auditioning, half is performing. Why stint on the auditioning half?

What to Say When You Won't Audition When You're Asked

Producer Stuart Ostrow saw a young actor, brand new to New York, do a role in an Off-Off-Broadway musical showcase. He asked me to have him in to audition for the title role in PIPPIN. The young actor didn't show up for the audition as scheduled. When I called his agent, I was told the actor had gone to see PIPPIN and didn't want to play that role. A dumb decision. If an actor has a chance to audition for Bob Fosse and Stuart Ostrow, he should. If he then decides he doesn't want the role, he should have the tact to say he's got another commitment, not insult the creators by saying he doesn't like their role. What does that attitude achieve, superiority for the actor? The people in a position to hire him *in the future* are offended—unnecessarily. Diplomacy is far better than candor, when the honesty hurts someone else who doesn't need or want your "honest" reaction. Actors, too, need to learn that candor is a highly valued commodity, to be used sparingly, only when it achieves a creative end.

It is understandable: actors get rejected so often that the desire for revenge is naturally a strong one. But it is without profit to the actor—the world of creating theatre and films is too small to afford offending. Better by far to be tactful and diplomatic when you turn down any job by saying you're doing so because of prior commitments, not because you don't like the role or the play or the project. The very next play by this same writer or producer or director may be the role you want more than any in your life.

Brief Observations That Might Be Useful

Actors decide to be strong in a scene. You can't "be strong," since that is an abstraction and difficult to fulfill. You can be strong *about* something: "I feel strongly that you should not get married"; "I feel strongly that your father is wrecking your life"; "I feel strongly that I love you."

Actors also decide a character is "weak" or "strong," which I think is a mistake. These are also generalizations that you can't act. We are all strong at times, weak at times; just as we are all masculine at times, feminine at times (even if the American behavior myth won't admit that). It is best to look for where you are strong or weak in the scene and *about what*, rather than make any judgment of character that is limiting.

Beware of all limitations. I am amazed when working on a play I've written that an actor will say to me, "But my character wouldn't do that," after the director or I have suggested some action to them. They say their character wouldn't do an action when I wrote the character? Something's wrong. The wrong is to decide on limitations; every "don't" choice you make cuts out a possible action.

Humor is a very handy action to use in order to break tension in a scene. That's why you needn't be afraid of going too far. Just as in life, when we go too far, we tend to laugh at ourselves. We laugh when someone else goes too far. Take the risk.

Allow yourself to be surprised at yourself. Actors leave this out. It's a common, natural life practice. Do it in the acting, too. It can be highly engaging.

When you feel yourself pushing an emotion in a scene to the point of artificiality, use that awareness. Use it the way you do in life, with a communication (not necessarily spoken aloud) to your partner: "My Lord, I'm being idiotic." We frequently admit that and go right on being idiotic. Or we may change and become rather sane. Or if you feel you're pushing, blame your partner: "Look what you're making me do! I never act like this other times."

Charm is useful. Since we use our charm to get what we want in life, it's amazing how few actors use their charm in a reading. Charm can be very productive. When the other person sees through it and feels you are insincere, you can charm them back by your sincerity.

When an actor upstages you, use it. The same way you would in life: register your awareness, with humor; then be willing to compete with him. Recently in a threesome reading of the three crazy ladies in Jean Giradoux's THE MAD WOMAN OF CHAILLOT, one actress took total attention by her use of an invisible parakeet on her little finger, talking to her imaginary characters, *and* relating to Dickie, the imaginary dog. The other actresses were wiped offstage, simply because they never dealt with what the inventive actress was doing. If they had competed, all three could have had fun, been interesting, and extended the relationships of the play, which are highly competitive. Most upstaging is not intentional in a reading situation; but even if it is, you can use it valuably.

Actors frequently tell me they are trying to create "anger" in a scene. Anger is caused by hurt. You must create the hurt and then you will find your reaction to the hurt, which may be anger; it may also be tears, breakdown, a cry for help, hysterics, insanity, humor, mystery and secret, immediate competition, any number of other actions. But *you cannot be angry unless you have been hurt*. Constantly I watch actors trying to create anger, wondering why they fail. They haven't created the hurt that causes it.

Think of the image you are creating when you dress for an audition. A little bit can help a lot. When I was working on the musical version of THE CORN IS GREEN with Josh Logan, we were both very excited by a talented newcomer named Dorian Harewood, but on the day Dorian auditioned for Miss Bette Davis, who was to star in the musical, he wore sophisticated, urban, prosperous clothing, looking his most handsome and worldly. Miss Davis understandably wondered where was the illiterate fieldhand whom she was to educate from ignorance to a chance at a scholarship to a fine northern university. Another actor was perilously close to being chosen for the role because Dorian hadn't changed his bright and shining image, until I persuaded Josh to get Miss Davis and Dorian together for a talk, just the two of them. After that meeting, Dorian got the role he so richly deserved, for Miss Davis is one very perceptive lady.

Don't believe what's written. The actor's job is to add dimension. Example: The minister father in SUMMER AND SMOKE is written as a put-upon bigot, defeated by his daughter and wife—not Tennessee Williams's most dimensional characterizing. But what is he fighting for? To give affection to his family, even though he never succeeds. He wants to forgive them for defying him, he wants to grant them freedom, but he is afraid, he lacks courage and independence. Actors are often misled by failure: what we fail to do may be exactly what we've always *wanted* to do. The fact that we don't get what we want doesn't negate its being a giant need in us.

Why does the mother in SUMMER AND SMOKE go loco? She can't get what she needs from either her husband or her daughter, she can't get through to them with a communication they can answer, so she retreats into a private world. The way of the crazy is frequently the admission of defeat at dealing with the world as it is. She creates a world that is as it *should* be: private and responsive only to her.

Both of these characters, so sketchily written, can be given dimension and poignancy by the actors who do them.

When actors have trouble finding humor in a scene, it's usually because they don't know what humor is. They think it's jokes rather than a way of dealing with problems. They hear me say, "Humor is our way of dealing with problems," and they think, "Huh? What does that mean? Humor always seemed to me to be having no problems." So I suggest they look at other people. It's a lot easier to see humor at work in other people than to see it in oneself. Watch closely during the next week. In life situations when there is a problem or a conflict, humor is almost invariably used by one person to overcome the hostility of the partner, smoothing it out and making it acceptable, coaxing him into finding a solution to the problem at hand. Watch where the *need* for humor comes in, because where you need humor in order to deal with problems is exactly where you can place humor in any scene you read. The humor is sometimes written into the scene, but very often it is not. It must be supplied by the actor out of his own life needs.

When an actor says, "I have a lot of trouble with cold readings," it is frequently because he is concerned with what *they* want rather than with what he is fighting for in the scene. The choices should come from his own life awareness, not from his efforts to please the auditors. There's no way of knowing what the auditors want! I'm with them all day at auditions, yet I frequently don't know what they want because they frequently don't know. They'll know it when they see it. Do your own thing, which is prescribed by the circumstances of the scene.

It's hard for an actor to trust he will get something useful from his partner (who may be an actor or a stage manager) in a reading. Getting what is termed "nothing" can be useful. Use it. It happens in life all the time that we get "nothing" we want from a relationship. If our needs are strong enough, that "nothing" will stimulate us to fight for what we do want.

The actor must always know more than the character does. The character does not know what is in his subconscious and yet he is deeply affected by, importantly motivated by, that dynamic. Thus the actor must *know* what the character does not consciously know.

One of the most important fantasies: this could be *the* relationship. This person is the one who could change my life. This could be what I've always been looking for. Dream a little. Make it a big dream.

Literary choices are not dramatic. Make your choices from emotional need rather than intellectual understanding.

If you are strongly connected to what you are fighting for and to the action you are determined to commit in the scene, you will be more open to making discoveries. Discoveries involve risk: what will you do with this new information?

When you really want to win and the stakes are life and death (literally, not figuratively), then you will take important risks.

Good friends do hurt each other. They can't be good friends if they don't. Good friends have been through the experience of hurting, yet they forgive each other. Forgiving is not the same as forgetting; it's a much deeper event.
Friendships are among the hardest relationships for actors to achieve. They forget the pain, they forget the competition, they forget the paying off: if you do this for me now, I'll do what you want later on when you want it.

Silence is a form of communication that is an alternative to verbal communication. Silence cannot be used by an actor as noncommunication. It is a way of *saying* something to someone else. *Silence is silent dialogue.*

Thus you must avoid dead spots. There can be no dead spots on stage. Everything must communicate. Every moment, every move, every silence must speak.

Mere reality is never enough. Neither is truth. It must be heightened reality, selective truth, made dramatic by the involving choices of the actor.

Whenever a character says he wants to go to sleep, that's not the action the actor should pick. I've spent too many times watching actors going to sleep or fighting to go to sleep onstage. My reaction now is: "Oh screw it, *go* to sleep! I'll go home and read a good book."

The action to pick is to *threaten* to go to sleep: see how I can punish you for not giving me what I want; but if you give me what I want, I'll wake up immediately. Give me what I want!

Being asleep onstage for an audition is not at all interesting.

Conflict, not contemplation, is dramatic truth. Save contemplation for philosophic essays or for sitting on the toilet all by yourself.

What is the point of falling half in love? Who's interested in that? A wishy-washy love affair, where the man isn't sure he's in love and the woman isn't needful of anything. If you pick falling in love, fall all the way: with a loud bang that can be heard even in Detroit. Go for broke.

Go for broke. Don't do the scene like an exploratory operation: It is life-and-death surgery.

The script is the best prop you can have in a reading. Hold on to the damn thing and use it to work *through*, or it will become a scene about an actor looking for a script.

Women seem to have more trouble than men in realizing that all their relationships with other women are competitive. They deny this fact. An actress would do well to know that all women compete with one another. The greatest of the Miss Goody Two-Shoes is as highly competitive as the meanest witch of them all. Competition is the life and breath of all relationships. Actresses: Accept competitiveness. Get right in there and compete. The Age of the Weaker Sex is long since gone (I doubt it ever existed).

Actors tend to be too polite to each other onstage in readings. Be polite offstage; I'm all for that. But onstage this "After you, Alphonse,"–"Oh no, you go first, Gaston!" attitude kills the competitive life of the audition. Onstage is where you must fight to the death, not defer.

I'm confounded by how fond actors are of playing with their partner's hair. Although the partner rarely protests—I would—neither does he or she evidence any fondness for the fondling. Such petting and smoothing and roughing up that goes on! I never notice people doing this in life; it seems to be an activity exclusive to actors. I presume it comes from a genuine effort to make contact with the other person in the scene, but it never rings true to me. I fear this activity may so distract the auditors that their attention may go to hair fondling rather than to the reality the actor is working so avidly to create. Instead of watching you, auditors sit highly aware of the discomforture of the person who's hair is being mauled, fearful that a wig may come off, a scar or even a bald lady will be revealed—something untoward that will embarrass us all.

Actors lose faith easily. I say: make a strong choice and go with it. To hell with whether it's right or wrong. The audition isn't about being right or wrong, it's about commitment. Actors are consumed with the fear of being wrong. Keep faith in your choice and plow right ahead; make a strong choice and *keep it strong*. If you have opposites of equal intensity, you're taking the right kind of risk.

Actors must learn to listen to what is said to them at auditions. When casting LOOT, readings were held on the set of another show where the only light source was on a far upstage platform. As actors came on to read, I told each of them where the only light was located. Eighty-seven percent of them came downstage, close to the foots, to read in the darkness. Is it that they don't listen or don't believe what they hear, or do they mistakenly believe that the closer they are to the auditors, the better their reading will be? It's time to learn that *the greater the distance between you and the person to whom you are communicating, the harder you will work to bridge that distance.*

If I ask enough questions of an actor, almost invariably he can do a better reading. Since I do not provide the answers, it must be clear that the actor has not been asking himself the right questions. Most actors can come up with the answers. So ask the questions!

Don't let yourself off the hook. Pursue the answers until they lead to more questions that require turmoil and the deepest parts of your awareness to answer. Acting hurts.

Most actors don't need enough from their partners. Need the most. The most love, the most response, the most belief, the most of whatever it is you want. Only the most will give you a reading of dimension.

If your partner does give you what you want, then want more. In life we always do.

Some actors are crazy for props. Can't live without them. Are hooked on them and need the fix every time they go near a stage. Most often props are not useful in an audition. They get in the way. You're not rehearsed, so you're not ready to use them.

Besides, how can you use props very successfully when you've got a script in hand? Pantomime whatever you need.

Pantomime props are for *your* use, and for you only. The auditors don't care because when you do the play, you'll have real props; your adeptness at pantomiming is of no interest to them. You're not auditioning for Marcel Marceau. So feel free: when you need a cocktail glass, have one; when you don't need it, let it disappear. You don't have to search for the proper vinyl-topped table to put it on, either; just let it go into thin air. I find it ridiculous to see an actor standing through a whole reading with his fingers up in the air holding an imaginary glass because his partner handed him one. It's for *you*, not for us. It's for the emotional use you can make of it, not to convince auditors you can be consistent in your use of props. That stuff is for classrooms, not for auditions.

Have faith in ESP. Everything doesn't need to be said aloud. If you try, with grave concentration, you can sometimes communicate by telepathy to another person. I've done it in life; so have you. Sometimes for experiment I do it in class: I try to *will* an instruction so strongly (during a reading) that the actor will do it. I say my message over and over, silently, sending the message with all my will toward the actor: Move to the left; move to the left; you're blocking yourself, so move to the left; get away from her; go to the left; make a strong move. Sometimes the actor actually does.

I find if you sense people strongly enough, you can affect them. A negative message doesn't get through, but a "do" message sometimes does. The sending of waves of energy toward your partner is bound to affect the airwaves. Even if your partner doesn't respond, he may be affected.

You know how often in life you are sitting next to someone when you suddenly turn to them and say, "What? What are you thinking?" You have been aware that they were sending you a strong message that they were not saying out loud.

Too much time is spent in the past, just as too much time is spent in analyzing. Try to make your decisions in the *now*, try to make what you are doing about today, not yesterday. Find immediacy. The impetus that drives you through the scene is what you are thinking and feeling *now*.

The audition is always now. That is why it is more like an improvisation, done just once, rather than a performance. The performance comes later, after you rehearse. Now is the audition. The audition is only now.

Your everyday life is not the criteria of what you are. Your fantasy life is who you are. Everybody's fantasy life is richer than reality.

An act of the imagination is what makes being alive possible.

Love is not always Romeo and Juliet. Most actors seem to think it is. Ideal love, or nothing, is how they view it.

Love is not always ideal. It takes very peculiar forms sometimes. Don't be so idealistic in your concepts. You overlook a lot of the strange places where love occurs, a lot of the strange, bizarre images that can be above love, too. The boy in EQUUS loves horses, prefers them to girls. The boy in ENTERTAINING MR. SLOANE loves an older man, an older woman, a young man, almost anyone who'll be handy to him. Who says it's not love?

If love had to have the romance, youth, and perfection of Romeo and his Juliet, most of us would never experience love at all.

Actors are too conventional. Love can be very odd, sometimes.

An actress was doing the final scene with Treplev in THE SEA GULL, which actresses dearly love to do. It's one of the most difficult in all theatredom, if not impossible, yet every actress worth her salt insists on trying it on for size. I asked this actress what was her image of a sea gull. "It's a bird that swoops down and picks up garbage out of the harbor," she told me.

No wonder she couldn't fulfill the romance of wanting to be a sea gull! Did she think of herself as the pig of the airways when she said, "I'm a sea gull!" What kind of romance can you create when you think of yourself as an eater of garbage.

It turned out that she had never seen a sea gull fly, with that incredible graceful wingspan, floating on the air the way they do.

There needs to be more floating on air in acting, less garbage.

Epilogue

Jed Harris was fond of naps. That elegant and brilliant American director told me that the secret of life was twelve-minute naps several times a day and to hell with wasting the entire night sleeping when there was so much else to do. As long as there was a fascinating and pretty lady unseduced, Mr. Harris was not about to waste a night in sleep. When he was very young, in his early twenties, Mr. Harris astonished the New York theatre by having four hit plays running simultaneously. Later on, Mr. Harris was bored with success. His shadow side was every bit as strong as his creative side, and it took over. He didn't really like work and would go to elaborate lengths to avoid it.

I was the production assistant when he directed the Sartre play RED GLOVES, which brought Charles Boyer for the first time to Broadway. Daniel Taradash was doing the adaptation, so he and Mr. Harris and I met regularly to struggle to get an American script that Mr. Harris felt he could direct. One day Mr. Harris announced that he could no longer work in New York. The vibrations were wrong. He hired a bed-sitting room on a train to Boston, so we could be isolated from the world of telephones and ladies. All the way to Boston he taught me to write upside down, which he said would come in handy in my future life. (Another time, on a different play, this one by Herman Wouk, the novelist, Mr. Harris took us to the Half Moon Hotel at Coney Island, deserted in the middle of a snowy winter, to work on the script away from the warmth of the bright lights of Manhattan. We spend half the first day going up and down in the elevator to various floors looking in vain for the dreamy room where Mr. Harris had once spent a glorious weekend with a glorious woman fifteen years earlier. When the Saturday came and I was scheduled to return to New York to pick up my Dalmatian, who was en route in a large crate on a train from Virginia, Mr. Harris took my shoes while I slept and had them locked in the hotel safe. Undeterred, I set out in my stocking feet through the snow until I found a taxi to take me back to New York to get my dog. My shoes may still be locked up in that hotel safe.)

When we got to Boston, we went to see José Ferrer starring in a Theatre Guild play that seemed to be taking place in an old people's home, for all I remember were dozens of very mature character actors. Someone had told Jed there was an actor in it perfect for RED GLOVES, but after forty-five minutes of watching the play, Jed decided rightfully that there wasn't, so we spent the rest of the play in the bar next door until time to pile back on our train for New York. We played gin rummy all the way back to New York. When we parted at dawn's early light, still not a word had been said about the script of RED GLOVES. Eventually, Dan and Jed did wrest a script from the Sartre, and RED GLOVES did get on the boards. Mr. Boyer was a success, but the play was not.

Mr. Harris was fond of testing scenes or lines on me. One night, he asked me what I thought of a bit he'd just suggested.

"Not much," said I, figuring I might as well be frank. I had not yet learned that if you are going to be frank to a creative person, you had better be tactful as well and have something highly positive to offer—or keep your bloody mouth shut.

"Not much?" asked Mr. Harris, noncommittally.

"Not much," I repeated, foolishly.

"You know," Mr. Harris said dreamily, leaning back to run his fingers up and down the venetian blind, "we can find kids on the street who aren't as fresh as you are. Get out of here."

I packed up my old kit bag and I went home. I had learned my lesson. Never again did I express an opinion to anyone for the rest of my life in the theatre unless I could offer something constructive, some way that might make it better. I set for myself a goal: I would never go to a play as a mere audience member, but as if I were a part of the creative staff who were putting that play on the boards. I would use every playgoing as a learning experience.

I advocate that to all actors—and to every director and writer and designer. Never be a *passive* audience. That's for civilians. Your job every time you go to the theatre, every time you go to the flicks, every turn on of that television set, is to put yourself in the shoes of those people who are acting, writing, directing. Find ways you can contribute to make what you're seeing better than it is.

That is why, in the classes I teach, I involve the entire class in every scene that is presented, force observers to articulate constructive criticism, push them into empathizing with every actor who appears before them. If there are ten scenes done in an evening's class, then each member can have ten opportunities to test his mettle, rather than one. Why do just your own one scene when you can gain the learning value from doing the other nine as well?

Every day, learn. Learn enough so that you can do good theatre.

Index

INVENTORY 1983